The Preacher's Struggle and Stamina

The Preacher's Struggle and Stamina

Insight from the Lives of the
Apostle Paul and
C. H. Spurgeon

including an "interview" with Spurgeon

Volume Two

by
Frank R. Shivers

Unless otherwise noted, Scripture quotations are from
The Holy Bible *King James Version*

Library of Congress Cataloging-in-Publication Data

Shivers, Frank R., 1949-
The Preacher's Struggle and Stamina Vol. 2 / Frank Shivers
ISBN 978-1-878127-51-8

Library of Congress Control Number:
2022922575

Cover design by
Tim King

For Information:
Frank Shivers Evangelistic Association
2005 Congress Road
Hopkins, South Carolina 29061
www.frankshivers.com

PRESENTED TO

_____

BY

_____

DATE

_____

"The man who realizes God's presence is by that
invisible companionship rendered invincible."[1]
~ C. H. Spurgeon

"[I pray] that we might not outlive our usefulness."[2]
~ David Brainerd

To the preacher

Who forsakes all for the sake of the call;

Who counts it a joy to suffer for Jesus' name's sake;

Who is thought a fool for his staunch biblical stance;

Who possesses a fire in his bones compelling him to preach;

Who snatches the lost as brands from the burning;

Who stands ready to do God's bidding at home or abroad;

Who preaches Christ crucified, resurrected, coming again;

Who 'the world is unworthy of' (Hebrews 11:38);

Who won't quit until the race is finished and the task is done.

Charles Spurgeon's Challenge to Pastors to Persevere

"If there be a hundred reasons for giving up your work of faith, there are fifty thousand for going on with it. Though there are many arguments for fainting, there are far more arguments for persevering. Though we might be weary, and do sometimes feel so, let us wait upon the Lord and renew our strength, and we shall mount up with wings as eagles, forget our weariness, and be strong in the Lord and in the power of his might."[3]

"As long as there is breath in our bodies, let us serve Christ; as long as we can think, as long as we can speak, as long as we can work, let us serve Him. Let us even serve Him with our last gasp; and, if it be possible, let us try to set some work going that will glorify Him when we are dead and gone. Let us scatter some seed that may spring up when we are sleeping beneath the hillock in the cemetery."[4]

"My inference from this saying of Christ, 'It is finished,' is this: has He finished His work for me? Then I must get to work for Him, and I must persevere until I finish my work, too—not to save myself, for that is all done, but because I am saved. Now I must work for Him with all my might; and if there come discouragements, if there come sufferings, if there comes a sense of weakness and exhaustion, yet let me not give way to it; but inasmuch as He pressed on till He could say, 'It is finished,' let me press on till I too shall be able to say, 'I have finished the work which Thou gavest me to do.'"[5]

"I give you the motto: 'Go forward.' Go forward in personal attainments, forward in gifts and in grace, forward in fitness for the work, and forward in conformity to the image of Jesus."[6]

"By perseverance, the snail reached the ark."[7]

Contents

Foreword

The prophet Daniel said, "The people that do know their God shall be strong, and do exploits." Anyone who fights a good fight for God will face the opposition of Satan and the world system of which he is the prince. There will be struggles calling for stamina on the part of the faithful servant of God.

Still, in every age God has raised up strong soldiers who have done "exploits." Two such men raised up by God were the Apostle Paul and Charles Haddon Spurgeon. Although they lived in widely separated eras and served in vastly different cultures, each performed mighty deeds for the God they knew and trusted supremely.

Evangelist Frank Shivers has drawn upon the wisdom of the inspired Apostle and the inspiring pastor to glean counsel for any minister who goes to battle for God and comes face to face with the inevitable opposition. Using the experiences and the expositions of these two giants, he has gleaned instruction that will enable the struggling preacher to maintain his stamina.

This two-volume set begins with a brief but illuminating biography of Charles Spurgeon. The author consulted many previous accounts of Spurgeon's life, some of which were penned shortly after his death by people who knew him personally. Although I was involved several years ago in producing a new edition of a large biography of this "prince of preachers," I came across much new information from these lesser-known works.

Also used were the words of Spurgeon himself from the multitude of sermons he preached that were published in full during and even after his lifetime. Spurgeon was very transparent in personal references and gave clear insights into his personal struggles. His well-known success gives testimony to his stamina in the face of these struggles, and he shows in his sermons what it was that enabled him to keep going—trust in the Word of God and reliance on the strength and faithfulness of God. These are the very things that will help us today to fight a good fight.

Volume two closes with a "literary interview with Charles Spurgeon." The author poses questions as an interviewer might, and lets the preacher answer with his own words drawn from his preaching and writings. It is a closing to this work that is as fitting and worthy as it is informative.

Frank Shivers has written numerous books drawing on his decades of ministry experience, seeking to leave behind helps for those who will take up the mantle. These volumes are valuable additions to that body of work and will serve the preacher well at whatever stage of ministry he may be in.

TERRY FRALA

Murfreesboro, TN

April 2024

Preface

My introduction to Charles Spurgeon was as a college freshman (1968) when I purchased seven books of his sermons from a classmate. The books, still on my shelf, prompted the further acquisition of his writings (like *Morning and Evening*, *Treasury of David*, *Lectures to My Students*, *The Soul Winner* and *An All-Round Ministry*) which have instructed, encouraged, and counseled me immensely. To say he has been to me a ministerial model and mentor throughout my ministry would be an understatement.

Not only have I been impacted by Spurgeon's sermons and books, but by his staunch perseverance in ministerial adversity and bodily affliction—how he coped with illnesses that plagued his body continually (nearly one-third of his last twenty-two years of life was spent absent from the pulpit suffering, convalescing, or taking precautions against the return of illness[8]), the debilitating sickness of his wife, Susannah, who was a virtual "shut-in" and the attacks of the liberal media, Baptist Union of Britain, and Christian antagonists of his day. Of his trials and pain, he wrote, "I have been cast into 'waters to swim in,' which, but for God's upholding hand, would have proved waters to drown in. I have endured tribulation from many flails."[9]

J. C. Carlile ends his biography of Spurgeon by saying, "The steady persistence and cheery optimism with which he faced difficulties are examples we cannot neglect. In times of depression, there is a real danger of accepting the spirit of defeat. May we not turn to Spurgeon as our guide, that perchance we may secure his tenacity of purpose and serenity of spirit?"[10]

The Apostle Paul and Spurgeon have in common not only their theology and passion for souls but their suffering, struggle, and stamina in Christian ministry (neither was bulletproof). Despite the hardships (though markedly different), they endured to the end, having fought a good fight each step of the way. Through the record of Paul in the Holy Scripture and the preservation of the writings of Spurgeon (sermons, memoirs, autobiography, biography, letters, diary, etc.) the minister is blessed with invaluable insights about persevering in adversity. It is my prayer that the insights gleaned from both men which are set forth in this two-volume set will assist the minister "to endure suffering (hardship) as a good soldier of the Lord Jesus Christ" until their sacred task is finished.

The two volumes are interlinked. Based upon the lives of the Apostle Paul and Charles Haddon Spurgeon, Volume One identifies the struggles and pain of the preacher (that which the minister may anticipate to large measure), and Volume Two presents principles that will help us endure and persevere. The first volume is the foundation for the second and includes a biography of Spurgeon.

The prayerful intent of both is to enable the minister to say with Spurgeon, "Now I must work for him with all my might; and if there come discouragements, if there come sufferings, if there comes a sense of weakness and exhaustion, yet let me not give way to it; but inasmuch as He pressed on till He could say, 'It is finished,' let me press on till I too shall be able to say, 'I have finished the work which thou gavest me to do.'"[11] Original or certifiable documentation of material used is cited (in most cases) to facilitate the reader's usage and research, and paraphrasing at large is avoided to display Spurgeon's oratory giftedness and anointing and to maintain the flavor, exactness, and force of that which he said.

While veteran preachers will find benefit from these books, they are aimed at ministerial students and those new to the pastorate. Respectfully, I urge all who choose to read them to bear that in mind. What may be found to be "meat" to a "raw recruit" (as Spurgeon called them) may be counted as "milk" to a master in Israel. With Spurgeon, I value the opportunity "to [humbly endeavor] to put the bread into the hands of the disciples [workers for God]," knowing "they will pass it on to the multitude."[12]

"He being dead, yet speaketh." Though the lifework of both Paul and Spurgeon has ended, they have left in the sand invaluable footprints for preachers to follow, not only to enhance their spiritual walk and work, but to navigate with both endurance and success the adversities that await (Revelation 14:13).

At the memorial service of C. H. Spurgeon for the public (February 10, 1892) Ira D. Sankey sang,

Fading away like the stars of the morning,
Losing their light in the glorious sun,
Thus would we pass from the earth and its toiling,
Only remembered by what we have done.

Shall we be missed though by others succeeded,
Reaping the fields we in springtime have sown?
No, for the sowers may pass from their labors,
Only remembered by what they have done.

Only the truth that in life we have spoken,
Only the seed that on earth we have sown,
These shall pass onward when we are forgotten,
Fruits of the harvest and what we have done.

Oh, when the Savior shall make up His jewels,
When the bright crowns of rejoicing are won,
Then shall His weary and faithful disciples
All be remembered by what they have done.

~ Horatius Bonar (1870)

"And they overcame him by the blood of the
Lamb and by the word of their testimony,
and they did not love their lives to the death."
(Revelation 12:11 NKJV)

1

Sustaining Grace

"May we be kept faithful by grace almighty, or the responsibility which rests upon us will grind us to powder!"[13]

~ C. H. Spurgeon

Principle: Grace enables the preacher to endure the direst of conditions, circumstances and calamities.

Grace molds the preacher into God's design to fit him for his divine assignment and provides whatever consolation and help are needed in the pilgrimage to Heaven. Grace is the bookends of the story of his life and work. Preserving (keeping) grace secures him from sin's power and penalty (Romans 5:21); sanctifying grace sets him apart for God's purpose of holiness and enables growth in Christlikeness, holy conduct, spiritual disciplines, and the knowledge of the Word (Hebrews 10:14; 1 Thessalonians 5:23); serving grace empowers the use of his spiritual gifts (Hebrews 12:28; 1 Peter 4:10; 1 Corinthians 12:4–31) to extend the kingdom of God (2 Corinthians 9:8; Acts 14:3); and sustaining grace is the supernatural help of God given in times of need, hardship, suffering, sorrow, trouble, sickness (2 Corinthians 12:8–9). "Let us, therefore, come boldly unto the throne of grace, that we may obtain mercy, and find grace to help in time of need" (Hebrews 4:16). If there's a secret to Paul's and Spurgeon's endurance in affliction and adversity in ministry, it is their utter dependence upon grace.

Christ assured Paul that the supply of His grace for the carrying out of his ministry, and in particular for the bearing of the pain and buffeting, would never run dry (2 Corinthians 12:9). Having that promise, he had the strength to endure all things (1 Corinthians 13:7) and to do all things to the glory of God (1 Corinthians 10:31).

Paul later encapsulated his own response to this promise of complete sufficiency: "I am strong enough to meet all circumstances through my union with him who strengthens me" (Philippians 4:13).[14]

So likewise did Spurgeon. In the sermon "Not Sufficient, and Yet Sufficient," he states: "Our sufficiency is of God; let us practically enjoy this truth. We are poor, leaking vessels, and the only way for us to keep full is to put our pitcher under the perpetual flow of boundless grace. Then, despite its leakage, the cup will always be full to the brim. 'Our sufficiency is of God.'"[15]

Further Spurgeon states, "Our warfare is with evil within us and around us, and we ought to be persuaded that we are able to get the victory and that we shall do so in the name of the Lord Jesus. We are not riding for a fall, but to win, and win we shall. The grace of God in its omnipotence is put forth for the overflow of evil in every form—hence the certainty of triumph."[16]

Grace enables the minister to endure fatigue, the bitterest storms, and the severest battles. Whatever comfort is needed, God's grace is sufficient to bestow; whatever the difficulty, His grace is sufficient to uphold; whatever the suffering, His grace is sufficient to sustain; whatever the fear, His grace is sufficient to subdue; whatever the anxiety, His grace is sufficient to calm; whatever the ministry, His grace is sufficient to accomplish; whatever the gloom, His grace is sufficient to dispel; and whatever the danger, His grace is sufficient to deliver. See Romans 5:3.

Saith Charles Simeon, "We should have it as a settled principle in our minds, that there is no strength in man, nor any other source of grace than Christ Jesus; and without hesitation we should go to Him from day to day, and from hour to hour, to receive it out of His fulness. He has told us that whatever be our necessities, 'his grace is sufficient for us'; therefore, instead of dreading trials lest we should be vanquished by them, we should 'take pleasure in them, that the power of Christ may rest upon us, and His strength be magnified in our weakness.'"[17]

Saith Spurgeon, "Are we just now called to some extraordinary service? Does the Lord lay upon us a heavy burden for His name? Do not let us shirk it or say, 'I cannot do it.' No; 'Lord, quicken thou me. Give me more grace, and then I shall be equal to any emergency, for as my days my strength shall be.'"[18]

"What matters it how much we suffer," says Spurgeon, "if we have grace to endure it? Put a believer where you will, if his Master gives him grace, he is in the best place he can be for security. I have heard brethren sometimes say that such a minister is in great danger; his position is lofty, his head will be turned. Ah! brethren, if he had had the keeping of his own head, it would have been turned long ago."[19]

In one of his last letters (1938), G. Campbell Morgan wrote, "I have found through all the sixty years that grace is sufficient, and I am quite sure it's never-failing grace, whatever life may bring, until earthly service merges into that of the life of the life Beyond."[20]

Saith Spurgeon: "When our troubles are many we are often by grace made courageous in serving our God; we feel that we have nothing to live for in this world, and we are driven, by hope of the world to come, to exhibit zeal, self-denial, and industry."[21]

The saints of Hebrews 11 epitomized grace amidst the worst of hardship, torture, and suffering, turning their weakness into strength, enabling them to persevere (Hebrews 11:34).

Horatius Bonar states, "The road is rugged, and the sun is hot. How can we be but weary? Here is grace for the weariness—grace which lifts us up and invigorates us, grace which keeps us from fainting by the way, grace which supplies us with manna from Heaven and with water from the smitten rock. We receive this grace and are revived. Our weariness of heart and limb departs. We need no other refreshments. This is enough. Whatever the way be—rough, gloomy, unpleasant— we press forward, knowing that the same grace that has already carried thousands through will do the same for us."[22]

James Smith (1860) gives a challenge to the minister: "Be strong in your *dependence upon* grace, and in your *expectations from* grace. Have no confidence in yourself; place no dependence on any creatures, but rely on divine grace alone. If you do so, you will be a match for all your *foes*, you will be fortified against all your *trials*, you will be furnished and prepared for all your *labors*, and you will be able to quench all the fiery darts of the Devil! Grace at first made us *Christians*, and grace must make us *conquerors*. As we *began* with grace, we must *go on* with grace, and at last we must *end* with grace. Our comfort, our encouragement, lies not in what we *are* or in what we can *do* or in what we *have*, but in what Christ is to us, and what Christ has for us. To Jesus, therefore, we must apply for all we need. To Jesus alone we must trust for grace to help us and to make us more than conquerors. We can do anything through grace—but we can do nothing without grace. Apart from Christ, we are weaker than an infant; but in Christ and through Christ, we are stronger than an archangel. Oh, for grace to teach us to be strong in the grace that is in Christ Jesus."[23]

Saith Chrysostom, "Not by our labor and industry, but by His grace."[24]

Let me but hear my Savior say,
"Strength shall be equal to the day,"
Then I rejoice in all distress,
Leaning on His sufficient grace.

I can do all things, or can bear
All sufferings, if my Lord be there;
Sweet pleasures mingle with the pains,
While His kind hand my soul sustains.

~ Isaac Watts (1674–1748)

> When God calls us to ministerial labor, we should endeavor to get grace that we may be strengthened into fitness for our position.
>
> Charles Spurgeon

Spurgeon, lecturing at the Pastor's College to aspiring young preachers, said, "When God calls us to ministerial labor, we should endeavor to get grace that we may be strengthened into fitness for our position and not be mere novices carried away by the temptations of Satan, to the injury of the church and our own ruin. We are to stand equipped with the whole armor of God, ready for feats of valor not expected of others; to us self-denial, self-forgetfulness, patience, perseverance, long-suffering must be everyday virtues, and who is sufficient for these things? We had need live very near to God if we would approve ourselves in our vocation."[25]

Grace has brought me safe this far,
And grace will lead me home.

~ John Newton (1779)

2

Bound by a Sacred Call

"I think it is no more possible to make a man cease from preaching, if he is really called, than to stop some mighty cataract [large waterfall] by trying, with an infant's cup, to drink its waters?"[26]

~ C. H. Spurgeon

> Principle: A fire in the soul to preach, kindled by the Holy Spirit, thwarts the preacher's quitting.

John Newton wrote, "None but He who made the world can make a minister of the Gospel."[27] Saith Martin Lloyd Jones, "Preachers are born, not made. This is an absolute. You will never teach a man to be a preacher if he is not already one."[28] And we who are ministers well understand why! (If God doth not make a man a minister, naught else can—education, training, parents, ability, charisma, etc.)

Saith Spurgeon, "No man may intrude into the sheepfold as an under-shepherd; he must have an eye to the chief Shepherd and wait his beck and command. Or ever a man stands forth as God's ambassador, he must wait for the call from above; and if he does not so, but rushes into the sacred office, the Lord will say of him and others like him, 'I sent them not, neither commanded them; therefore, they shall not profit this people at all, saith the Lord (Jeremiah 23:32).'"[29]

In the sermon "The Minister's Trumpet Blast and Church Member's Warning," Spurgeon states, "A true minister of Christ should know how to blow the ram's horn so that the walls of Jericho may be made to tremble and fall; he should understand how to play the harp so that when any of you are disquieted he may be to you as David was to Saul and may drive away the evil spirit that troubles you. He should be able, too, to play on the tambourine and to lead you out, sometimes, in the sacred song of joy and thanksgiving; he should be able to go out like Miriam and cry aloud to you and ask you to follow him while he says, 'Sing to the Lord, for he has triumphed gloriously.' His sermons should often seem to you to fulfil that exhortation of David: 'Praise the Lord. Praise him on the loud cymbals: praise him on the high-sounding cymbals.' The minister of the Gospel should understand also how to blow the silver trumpet to proclaim that the year of jubilee is come and that the ransomed debtors may once more receive their lost inheritance. And there is one instrument on which he should be well skilled, and which he should often use; namely, the trumpet. I do not mean the silver trumpet, but the war trumpet—that clear, shrill-sounding instrument that gives the certain sound by which men prepare themselves for the battle"[30] (Hosea 8:1–2). Paul concurs, saying, "For if the trumpet give an uncertain sound, who shall prepare himself to the battle?" (1 Corinthians 14:8).

Augustine said, "The ministry is a weight from which even an angel might shrink."[31] And certainly mortal man would if has not been divinely called to the task! The grappling hook of a heavenly call keeps ministers faithful to it when all that is in them says quit. They have been approved, authorized, and allowed "by God to be entrusted with the gospel" (1 Thessalonians 2:4 NKJV), and refuse to dishonor and disappoint Him.

Paul says, "God, with his mercy, gave us this work to do, so we don't give up" (2 Corinthians 4:1 NCV). Again, he testified, "I am compelled to preach [necessity is laid upon me]—and woe to me if I do not preach the gospel!" (1 Corinthians 9:16 CSB). "A vow was upon him; and there was no discharge, no intermission until his fight was fought and his course was run."[32]

> Draw a circle around my pulpit, and you have hit the spot where I am nearest Heaven.
>
> C. H. Spurgeon

Spurgeon made that vow and knew that same constraint, as do all who are truly called. "What is that necessity which is laid upon us to preach the Gospel?" asks the "Prince of Preachers." "First, a very great part of that necessity springs from the call itself. If a man be truly called of God to the ministry, I will defy him to withhold himself from it. A man who has really within him the inspiration of the Holy Ghost calling him to preach cannot help it. He must preach. As fire within the bones, so will that influence be until it blazes forth. Friends may check him, foes criticize him, despisers sneer at him; the man is indomitable. He must preach if he has the call of Heaven. All earth might forsake him, but he would preach to the barren mountaintops. If he has the call of Heaven, if he has no congregation, he would preach to the rippling waterfalls and let the brooks hear his voice. He could not be silent."[33]

Spurgeon found time preaching in the pulpit the sweetest delight of life. Saith he, "Draw a circle around my pulpit, and you have hit the spot where I am nearest Heaven. There the Lord has been more consciously near me than anywhere else. He has ravished my heart while I have been trying to cheer and comfort his mourners."[34] With that, the preacher well identifies.

Preachers are divinely gifted and chosen vessels to "preach," and preach they must. Joel Beeke advises, "Let every preacher take note: Amid the frustrations and hardships of ministry, the most Christ-like thing is to stay focused on your calling, give thanks to God, and go on preaching the Gospel."[35]

Erwin Lutzer wrote, "Some ministers scarcely have two good days back-to-back. They are sustained by the knowledge that God has placed them where they are. Ministers without such a conviction often lack courage and carry their resignation letter in their coat pocket. At the slightest hint of difficulty, they're gone."[36]

Charles Bridges states, "To labor in the dark, without an assured commission, greatly obscures the warrant of faith in the Divine engagements; and the minister, unable to avail himself of heavenly support, feels his 'hands hang down, and his knees feeble' in his work. On the other hand, the confidence that he is acting in obedience to the call of God—

that he is in His work, and in His way—nerves him in the midst of all difficulty, and under a sense of his responsible obligations, with almighty strength."[37]

The minister's call is increasingly more challenging. Firm stamina is required. Spurgeon sadly observed toward the end of his life that the outpouring of the Spirit he knew bountifully in the early years of ministry was declining. He writes, "Thirty years ago, things were very different from what they are now. It was easy to gather a congregation then, compared with what it is now; the spirit of hearing is departing from our cities."[38]

In 1887 he wrote, "We are going downhill at a break-neck speed."[39] And that which he witnessed at the close of the 19th century is even more prevalent in the 21st. Like Spurgeon, if you are sovereignly called to be a preacher, "be thou faithful unto death" (Revelation 2:10) despite ministry difficulty or decline.

Their conversion experience was also an impetus to endurance for both Paul and Spurgeon. Paul never forgot what happened on the Damascus Road (a road from Jerusalem to Damascus that stretches about 140 miles), and Spurgeon always remembered that which happened in a Primitive Methodist Chapel on January 6, 1850, in Colchester, England. An eternal debt of love and devotion to Christ for saving them compelled them not to quit. See Romans 8:12.

"Beloved brethren," appeals Spurgeon, "we are bound to go forward, cost us what it may, for we dare not go back; we have no armor for our backs. We believe ourselves to be called to the ministry, and we cannot be false to the call."[40] James Sherman sums up well the reason that neither Paul nor Spurgeon quit their sacred commission. He states, "Should it not excite us to perseverance when we think that Christ our Master has entrusted His cause in our hands? Who are we, that the Lord of all should let us labor for Him?"[41]

3
Power of Prayer

"Power in prayer is very much the gauge of our spiritual condition; and when that is secured to us in a high degree, we are favored as to all other matters."[42]

~ C. H. Spurgeon

Principle: Prayer prevents faltering and stumbling in Christian service.

The endurance exhibited by Paul and Spurgeon in trials may be inextricably linked to their passionate prayer life. Paul prayed "night and day" (2 Timothy 1:3), and Spurgeon declared that seldom did many minutes pass without him either praying or praising God.[43]

"We must always," says Spurgeon, "be in the spirit of prayer. Our heart must be like the magnetic needle, which always has an inclination towards the pole."[44] He states, "I cannot help praying. Minute by minute, moment by moment, somehow or other, my heart must commune with God. Prayer has become as essential to me as the heaving of my lungs and the beating of my pulse";[45] and, "I bear my testimony that there is no joy to be found in all this world like that of sweet communion with Christ. I would barter all else there is of Heaven for that. Indeed, that is Heaven. As for the harps of gold and the streets like clear glass and the songs of seraphs and the shouts of the redeemed, one could very well give all these up, counting them as a drop in a bucket, if we might forever live in fellowship and communion with Jesus."[46] Amen and amen.

But Spurgeon just didn't pray; he prayed with great earnestness and power. It was said of Spurgeon that his prayers raised up more of the sick than the treatments of any doctor in London.[47] Susannah and William Harrald, in *From the Pulpit to the Palm-Branch,* wrote, "He had many answers to prayer.

The record of his answered prayers would, of itself, fill a volume."[48]

One evening in a Tabernacle service, a man testified, "Mr. Spurgeon prayed with me this morning. I have been divinely healed." Doctors that very day had diagnosed his condition as critical.[49] Another man for years limped to the services at the church due to a partial paralysis. He entered the church and walked down the aisle decidedly and steadily to the front seat. The man had been healed when Spurgeon prayed for him.[50]

"A minister may fill his pews," says John Owen, "his communion roll, the mouths of the public, but what that minister is on his knees in secret before God Almighty, that he is and no more."[51] Saith Spurgeon, "I never met with a half-hearted preacher who was much in communion with the Lord Jesus."[52]

Intimacy with Christ affords an inner strength (stamina) that propels us forward in facing hindering headwinds (ministerial struggles, difficulties, persecution, and fatigue) without straying off course or sinking altogether (Hebrews 6:1; 1 Corinthians 10:12). It enabled Enoch to persevere in ministry (Jude 14) despite the vile and evil day in which he lived for 365 years.

Spurgeon wrote, "All our libraries and studies are mere emptiness compared with our closets. We grow, we wax mighty, we prevail in private prayer. The closet is the best study. The commentators are good instructors, but the Author himself is far better, and prayer makes a direct appeal to Him and enlists Him in our cause."[53] Saith Spurgeon, "If there be any man under Heaven who is compelled to carry out the precept 'pray without ceasing,' surely it is the Christian minister."[54]

Lecturing to aspiring preachers at the Pastor's College, he sounded that same note: "There should be special seasons for devotion, and it is well to maintain them with regularity; but the spirit of prayer is even better than the habit of prayer: to pray without ceasing is better than praying at intervals. It will be a happy circumstance if we can frequently bow the knee with devout brethren, and I think it ought to be a rule with us ministers never to separate without a word of prayer."[55] In the sermon "The Secret of Power in Prayer," he said, "The prevailer in prayer is the man to preach successfully, for he may well prevail with man for God when he has already prevailed with God for men."[56]

> The prevailer in prayer is the man to preach successfully, for he may well prevail with man for God when he has already prevailed with God for men.
>
> Charles Spurgeon

In the sermon "Do You Know Him?" Spurgeon reveals the importance of communion time with the Lord: "My soul, never be satisfied within a shadowy Christ. I cannot know Christ through another person's brains. I cannot love Him with another man's heart, and I cannot see Him with another man's eyes. I am so afraid of living in a second-hand religion. Lord, save us from having borrowed communion. No, I must know Him myself. O God, let me not be deceived in this. I must know Him on my own account."[57] "I must take care above all that I cultivate communion with Christ, for though that can never be the basis of my peace—mark that—yet it will be the channel of it."[58]

Charles Cook was saved under the ministry of Spurgeon's son Thomas, attended the Pastor's College, and published a selection of Spurgeon's prayers. He observes, "Spurgeon's power did not lie wholly in his exceptional preaching gifts. He was a mighty man of prayer. Not even his pulpit genius could have attracted such vast congregations throughout a period of nearly forty years, nor would his ministry have been so rich in spiritual results, had he not lived in closest intimacy with the unseen. 'You spoke as if you had come straight from the Presence,' said a worshiper on one occasion to Alexander Whyte. That was how many felt whenever Spurgeon preached."[59]

But Spurgeon also relied upon the prayer of the saints to enable his perseverance and power. In the sermon "The Statute of David for the Sharing of the Spoil," he said, "To me it is a boundless solace that I live in the prayers of thousands! I will not say which does the better service—the man that preaches or the man that prays—but I know this, that we can do better without the voice that preaches than without the heart that prays."[60] And in his autobiography he writes, "I always give all the glory to God, but I do not forget that He gave me the privilege of ministering from the first to a praying people. We had prayer meetings that moved our very souls; each one appeared determined to storm the Celestial City by the might of intercession."[61]

"It is a great sin," he said, "on the part of church members if they do not daily sustain their pastor by their prayers!"[62] In a sermon preached at Music Hall/Royal Surrey Gardens, on June 28, 1857, Spurgeon said, "Let me know when you give up praying for me, for then I must give up preaching, and I must cry, 'O my God, take me home, for my work is done!'"[63]

Spurgeon warns of dangerous ministerialism: "The worst [snare a minister can face] is the temptation to ministerialism— the tendency to read our Bibles as ministers, to pray as ministers, to get into doing the whole of our religion as not ourselves personally, but only relatively concerned in it [cold formality]."[64]

It would be unseemly to leave this chapter without mentioning the eloquence and power of Spurgeon's pulpit prayer which impressed the famed evangelist D. L. Moody more than his sermons did. Dinsdale Young, a contemporary of Spurgeon who heard many of Spurgeon's pulpit prayers, said, "He lived so entirely in the spiritual world that he was ever ready to pray. He had not to school himself at the moment. His pulpit prayers were not art, but nature. Every prayer was the effluence of a consecrated personality. No liturgy could have restrained him. One could not imagine him making literary preparation for public prayer. *The flower gave out its perfume without effort.* The urn was ever being filled where the pure waters rise, and so afforded at any moment abundant refreshment. Mr. Spurgeon loved God with his 'mind,' and our minds were stimulated when we heard him pray. The quivering sympathy of Mr. Spurgeon's prayers thrilled all who heard them. You felt the throbbing of that mighty heart."[65]

And of Spurgeon's pastoral prayers A. C. Dixon said, "And, oh, what praying, peculiar for that element of adoration in which nearly all public prayer is lacking! His confession of sin is humble, his supplication fervent, his intercession importunate; but when he praises and extols God, it is an eagle soaring toward the sun and bearing you on its wings. You see the glory of God; you feel smitten with the splendor of His power and wisdom, goodness and holiness."[66]

4

The Love of Christ

"For the love of Christ constraineth us; because we thus judge, that if one died for all, then were all dead."

~ The Apostle Paul (2 Corinthians 5:14)

Principle: The changeless love of God compels the preacher's faithfulness to the end.

John MacArthur says, "Christ's loving, substitutionary death motivated Paul's service for Him."[67] Pain, suffering, hardship, conflict, and fears exhaust our strength and threaten our faith. But knowing the love that Christ has for us ought to incite us not to back down or give up (2 Corinthians 5:14).

"Nothing grips a man," writes C. E. Autrey, "like love. One will endure hardships, cross oceans, suffer intimations, and even death, for love."[68] Christ's love for Paul moved him to endure beatings, stoning, imprisonment, and bitter ridicule for the sake of the call. It was the impetus that kept him going and faithful "in season, out of season." In the sermon "Under Constraint," Spurgeon says, "Every Christian minister ought to be able to use the apostle's words ["the love of Christ compels us"] without the slightest reserve."[69]

Alexander Maclaren said, "There must be the recognition of His death as the great sacrifice and sign of His love to us. The center of Christ's power over men's hearts is to be found in the fact that He died on the Cross for each of us."[70] Saith John Chrysostom, "By the cross we know the gravity of sin and the greatness of God's love toward us."[71] Where the love of Christ is known, self is dethroned, and Christ rules as King. Where this love is known, the heart loves back freely and fully. "We love Him, because He first loved us." Where this love is known, gratitude compels the heart to serve Him loyally and royally until death. Where this love is known, an indebtedness is felt to Christ that must be repaid.

Alexander Maclaren states, "Every servant of Jesus Christ who has received the truth for himself has received it as a steward, and is, as such, indebted to God, from whom he got the trust, and to the men for whom he got it. We are not at liberty to choose whether we shall do our part in spreading the name of Jesus Christ. It is a debt that we owe to God and to men."[72]

Spurgeon remarked, "Christ has paid the debt His people owed. I am a debtor to God's love, I am a debtor to God's grace, I am a debtor to God's power, I am a debtor to God's forgiving mercy, but I am no debtor to His justice—for He Himself will never accuse me of a debt once paid. But then because we are not debtors to God in that sense [justice], we become ten times more debtors to God than we should have been otherwise. Because He has remitted all our debt of sin, we are all the more indebted to Him in another sense. Consider how much you owe to His forgiving grace, that after ten thousand affronts He loves you as infinitely as ever; and after a myriad of sins, His Spirit still resides within you."[73] Amen!

Where this love of Christ has been truly experienced, the soul is constrained to "endure hardship as a good soldier of Jesus Christ" (2 Timothy 2:3 NKJV). Where this love is known, it will manifest itself to others. Where this love of Christ is known, it will move the heart to act as He acted. Where this wondrous love is known, boldness is displayed to preach the whole counsel of God. And where this love is known, it keeps the minister "employed" in Christ's service. "We are led to diligence," says Spurgeon, "urged to zeal, maintained in perseverance, and carried forward and onward by the love of Jesus Christ. The apostles labored much, but all their labor sprang from the impulse of the love of Jesus Christ. They could no more cease to preach than the sun could cease shining or reverse his course in the heavens."[74]

> *Nothing binds me to my Lord like a*
> *strong belief in His changeless love.*
> *C. H. Spurgeon*

What love is this that moves Paul and Spurgeon to suffer grave hardships for the Gospel and endure to the end? Spurgeon answers, "Herein is love indeed, that the infinitely pure should suffer for the sinful, the just for the unjust, to bring us to God. Love did never climb to so sublime a height as when it brought Jesus to the bloody tree to bear the dread sentence of an inexorable law. Think of this love, beloved, till you feel its constraining influence. It was love most persevering, for when man was born into the world and sinned and rejected Christ, and He came to His own and His own received Him not, He loved them still, loved them even to the end."[75] Further, Spurgeon testified, "Nothing binds me to my Lord like a strong belief in His changeless love."[76]

> Oh, love of God, how rich and pure!
> How measureless and strong!
> It shall forevermore endure,
> The saints' and angels' song.
>
> ~ Frederick Martin Lehman (1917)

A. W. Pink says, "It is important that the saint [minister] should make it his paramount concern to be more and more absorbed with the love of Christ, exercising his mind thereon, feeding his soul therefrom, delighting his heart therein, praying earnestly that he may more fully understand the love of God. He should attentively consider the revelation given of it in the Word of truth, meditating on its ineffable characteristics, contemplating its wondrous manifestations, and realizing that Christ's love to His own is eternal, infinite, and unalterable—not only without cessation but without the least diminution. Nothing will so much excite gratitude in his heart as a contemplation of the love of Christ to such an unlovely creature as he. Nothing will prompt so effectually to a life of self-denial. Nothing will make so pleasant and easy a walk of obedience to God. Nothing will so deaden the saint to the world. Nothing else can so fill him with peace, yes, and with joy, in a season of affliction or bereavement."[77]

Christ's love compels us to magnify and glorify Him by our unwavering obedience, sacrifice, and ministry. When questioned as to why you endure the anguish and agony of ministerial work, answer with Paul, 'The love of Christ constraineth me.' Saith Spurgeon, "You for whom Jesus has done little, if any such there be, love Him little; but I do beseech you—those of you whom He has loved with an extraordinary affection and who feel that you owe much to His grace, that He has done 'great things for you, whereof you are glad'—do not be content with doing what other people do. Think of others thus. 'I have no doubt that what they do is their best, but I must do more than they, for I owe Him more than they do.' And oh! if every one of us could feel this, we should account labor light and pain easy, and be disgusted with ourselves that we spend so much of our lives doing nothing for Him who has bought us with His most precious blood."[78]

Love of God, so pure and changeless!
Blood of Christ, so rich and free!
Grace of God, so strong and boundless!
Magnify them all in me.

~ Elizabeth Codner (1860)

"Keep yourselves in the love of God" (Jude 21). John Edwards remarked, "If they would be steadfast in their religion, they must embrace it out of love."[79]

5
Readiness to Suffer

"It takes away a thousand ills if we are ready for service, ready for suffering, ready to die."[80]

~ C. H. Spurgeon

Principle: Expectation of and readiness for adversity in ministry enables its endurance.

The Holy Spirit testified to Paul that "in every city… imprisonment and persecutions" were waiting for him (Acts 20:23 NRSV; see Acts 9:16). (How about hearing that as a young preacher starting out?) Undaunted by the news, Paul said in Romans 1:15, "I am ready" (specifically regarding going to Rome with the Gospel, but applicable to every hostile venue). And history proves that he was "ready" in mind and soul. Girded with the Word of God and the Sword of the Spirit (and the rest of the armor of God, Ephesians 6:10–18), he boldly withstood the adversity and affliction that came with the territory as a minister of God.

Paul may have used the words "I am ready" as his life motto, and if so, it would have been most fitting.[81] Saith Spurgeon, "He was no sooner converted, than he was ready for holy service; and 'straightway he preached Christ' in the synagogues at Damascus. All through his life, whatever happened to him, he was always ready. If he had to speak to crowds in the street, he had the fitting word; or if to the elite upon Mars' hill, he was ready for the philosophers. If he talked to the Pharisees, he knew how to address them; and when he was brought before the Sanhedrim and perceived the Pharisaic and Sadducean elements in it, he knew how to avail himself of their mutual jealousies to help his own escape. See him before Felix, before Festus, before Agrippa—he is always ready; and when he came to stand before Nero, God was with him and delivered him out of the mouth of the lion. If you find him on board ship, he is ready to comfort men in the storm; and when he gets on shore, a shipwrecked prisoner, he is ready to gather sticks, to help make the fires. At all points he is an all-round man and an all-ready man—always ready to go wherever his Master sends him and to do whatever his Lord appoints him."[82] Paul's readiness to suffer (not just expecta-tion of hardship) kept him in the ministry. See 2 Timothy 2:3.

> Ready to suffer grief or pain,
> Ready to stand the test;
> Ready to stay at home and send
> Others if He sees best.

Ready to go, ready to stay,
Ready my place to fill;
Ready for service lowly or great,
Ready to do His will.

~ A. C. Palmer (1845–1882)

What helped Paul be ready to suffer without fainting? Spurgeon answers, "He belonged to Christ. He was Jesus Christ's branded slave, and he was absolutely at Christ's disposal. Moreover, he had such trust in his Lord that he felt, *whatever he does with me, it will be good and kind, and therefore I will make no condition, I will have no reserve from him; it is the Lord, let him do what seemeth him good.* He had resolved to serve his Lord; and, therefore, if he had to be bound, or die, he would not shrink back."[83]

"You have not come to the highest style of readiness," says Spurgeon, "till you are ready for whatever the will of God may appoint for you. Unreadiness from this point of view is very common, but it shows unsubdued human nature. It is a relic of rebellion, for when we are fully sanctified, when every thought is brought into subjection to the mind of God, then the cry is not, 'As I will,' but 'As Thou wilt.'"[84]

Spurgeon, like Paul, practiced this readiness to suffer at the hands of scoffers, mockers, slanderers, and the religious liberal until his death. Prepare to be ready to stand firm and immovable in the faith. "Say 'Yes' before your fears have time to shape 'No.' Say 'No' before your inclinations have time to whisper 'Yes.'"[85]

Paul challenges, "Endure suffering along with me, as a good soldier of Christ Jesus" (2 Timothy 2:3 NLT). Suffering and pain await all who march into Hell for a heavenly cause (sometimes from family and friends). Be forewarned. Be ready. Gird thyself with the full gospel armor, lest you *faint* or *turn back* in the day of battle (Psalm 78:9).

See 1 Corinthians 15:58. Frame your life and ministry around the motto, "I am ready."

6
Not to Be Found Wanting

"I must be altogether weighed in the scales. I cannot hope that God will weigh my head and pass over my heart—that because I have correct notions of doctrine, therefore He will forget that my heart is impure, or my hands guilty of iniquity. My all must be cast into the scales."[86]

~ C. H. Spurgeon

> Principle: Fear of disqualification for ministry presently and future judgment provides an incentive for perseverance in holiness and ministry.

As a minister (runner in the race of life), Paul had accomplished much—thousands of converts and disciples, thirteen Bible books, three missionary journeys that expanded the kingdom—and he possessed an extensive and powerful influence among kings and paupers. All this he realized would be "loss" (not loss of salvation) through a "rule" infraction (1 Corinthians 9:27; 1 Timothy 3:2; Titus 1:6), if he was slothful in spiritual discipline—failure to knock out fleshly impulses that would hinder his mission.[87]

D. K. Lowery suggests, "Like the brother who had indulged in immorality (1 Corinthians 5:1–5), Paul's life could be cut short by the disciplinary disapproval of God."[88] All this he feared and took steps to prevent it. Thus, Paul said, "So I run with purpose in every step. I am not just shadowboxing. I discipline my body like an athlete, training it to do what it should. Otherwise, I fear that after preaching to others I myself might be *disqualified*" (1 Corinthians 9:26–27 NLT).

Saith Donald Grey Barnhouse, "Godly fear made him live like a runner in a race, hurling himself toward the goal with no thought of any other circumstance."[89] Matthew Henry says, "A holy fear of himself was necessary to preserve the fidelity of an apostle, and how much more necessary is it to our preservation?"[90] Holy fear of ourselves, and not presumptuous confidence, is the best security against becoming a castaway.[91]

> Godly fear made him live like a runner in a race, hurling himself toward the goal with no thought of any other circumstance.
>
> Donald Grey Barnhouse

Further, Paul's knowing that violation of the "rules" would result in God's disapproval, disqualification, and loss of reward incited him not to "faint." He writes, "Each one's work will be clearly shown [for what it is]; for the day [of judgment] will disclose it, because it is to be revealed with fire, and the fire will test the quality and character and worth of each person's work. If any person's work which he has built [on this foundation, that is, any outcome of his effort] remains [and survives this test], he will receive a reward. But if any person's work is burned up [by the test], he will suffer the loss [of his reward]; yet he himself will be saved, but only as [one who has barely escaped] through fire" (1 Corinthians 3:13–15 AMP). See 2 Corinthians 5:10.

Saith Alexander Maclaren, "He shall lose, in that he will stand further from the Lord, and possess, because he can contain, less of His glory. His crown is far less resplendent than the others; His seat at Christ's table in the kingdom is far lower. His Heaven is narrower and less radiant. These two are like two vessels, one of which comes into the harbor with a rich freight and flying colors and is welcomed with the tumult of acclaim. The other strikes the bar. 'Some on boards, and some on broken pieces of the ship, all come safe to land.' But ship and cargo and profit of the venture are all lost. 'He shall suffer loss, but he himself shall be saved.'"[92]

Spurgeon, in the sermon "The Heavenly Race," says, "You must keep to the course; you must keep straight on; you must not stop on the road or turn aside from it, but urged on by Divine grace, you must ever fly onwards 'like an arrow from the bow, shot by an archer strong.' And never rest until the march is ended and you are made pillars in the house of your God."[93]

To grasp the fact that our sermons, soul-winning, study, steadfastness, stand, service, and sins will be judged at the feet of Him who not only saved us but called us to ministry ought to compel the necessary discipline to work harder, honorably, passionately, and perseveringly, despite the struggle or hardship.

Speaking to a gathering of preachers, Spurgeon remarked, "It will matter eternally how we have discharged our work during our lifetime. 'Thou art weighed in the balances and art found wanting'—will that be the verdict on any one of us when we stand before the Lord God Almighty who trieth the hearts and searcheth the reins of the children of men? May we be kept faithful by grace almighty, or the responsibility which rests upon us will grind us to powder."[94]

And in the sermon "The King's Weighings," he hammers the point home further, saying, "The preacher here is being daily weighed, and he knows it; and however excellent our outward lives may be, we must still pass through the testing-house. Not one of us shall escape from the upright judgment of the Most High. And one day, to conclude this point, the King's weighings will be published—set up where men and angels shall read them. Oh, can you bear it that the whole of the secrets of your soul should be made public in the marketplace of the universe, that the actions which seemed so admirable should have their secret motives searched out and should be seen to be leprous with selfishness? Can you endure to have your secret sins laid bare; your private designs, deep intentions, and evil purposes set out in the open daylight? Can you bear to have your envying, jealousies, plotting, lying—all held up to public gaze?"[95]

Saith Spurgeon, "Paul was saved, and he knew it; and some of us know, to a certainty, that we are saved; but we also know that there is another crown to be won, which the Lord will give to His servants who win in the great fight with sin. To win this crown is our high ambition, and we long to hear the Master say to each one of us on that day, 'Well done, thou good and faithful servant; thou hast been faithful over a few things, I will make thee ruler over many things. Enter thou into the joy of thy Lord.'"[96] To receive the approval of God, a "W.D. degree" at the finish line, is a huge incentive not to faint or falter.

Adoniram Judson challenges, "A life once spent is irrevocable. It will remain to be contemplated through eternity.…If it has been a useless life, it can never be improved. Such will stand forever and ever. The same may be said of each day. When it is once past, it is gone forever. All the marks which we put upon it, it will exhibit forever.…Each day will not only be a witness of our conduct, but will affect our everlasting destiny [Not in loss of salvation but of rewards]. No day will lose its share of influence in determining where shall be our seat in Heaven. How shall we then wish to see each day marked with usefulness! It will then be too late to mend its appearance. It is too late to mend the days that are past. The future is in our power. Let us then, each morning, resolve to send the day into eternity in such a garb as we shall wish it to wear forever. And at night let us reflect that one more day is irrevocably gone, indelibly marked."[97]

There it will hurt like a wounding dart
When this dread answer shall fall;
Weighed and found wanting—'twill pierce thy heart
At the last judgment call.

~ Barney E. Warren (1907)

Pastors "keep watch over your souls *as those who will give an account.* Let them do this with joy and not with grief, for this would be unprofitable for you" (Hebrews 13:17 NASB). Matthew Henry comments, "They must give an account of how they have discharged their duty. If they can then give an account of their own fidelity and success, it will be a joyful day to them; those souls that have been converted and confirmed under their ministry will be their joy and their crown in the day of the Lord Jesus. If they give up their account with grief, it will be the people's loss as well as theirs."[98]

"The sight of the crown," saith Spurgeon, "removes all weight from our crosses. The race ceases to be severe when we see Jesus enthroned. I see Him today at the end of the course holding out the wreath to me and saying, 'He that shall endure unto the end, the same shall be saved.' Oh, that you may each one see Him and feel that 'the crown of glory that fades not away' is worthy of a life's running."[99]

Look up, my brother, "redemption draweth nigh." Soon the King will appear to take you Home. Stay focused. Guard each step. Don't get disqualified. Don't blemish the good accomplished. Don't become a castaway (1 Corinthians 9:27). Finish well, that you may attest with Paul, "I have fought a good fight, I have finished my course, I have kept the faith: Henceforth there is laid up for me a crown of righteousness, which the Lord, the righteous judge, shall give me at that day: and not to me only, but unto all them also that love his appearing" (2 Timothy 4:7–8).

Jonathan Edwards exhorts, "Hold fast and preserve that which *you* have. Continue in grace and persist in the ways of virtue, through all opposition. Cleave to the Rock of Ages, and you shall stand immovable; rely on Him, and you shall be upheld; depend on His promises, and you shall never fall."[100] Jesus said, "Behold, I come quickly: hold that fast which thou hast, that no man take thy crown" (Revelation 3:11). Hold fast to thy sacred trust in ministry, lest a Paul must say to you, "Ye did run well; who did hinder you that ye should not obey the truth?" (Galatians 5:7).

7
Royal Care of Family

"Let the husband love his wife as he loves himself, and a little better, for she is his better half. He should feel, If there's only one good wife in the whole world, I've got her."[101]

~ C. H. Spurgeon

Principle: Family devotedness must not be sacrificed on the altar of ministry.

Though Paul wasn't married, he gave husbands, through the inspiration of the Holy Spirit, great advice: "Husbands, love your wives, even as Christ also loved the church, and gave Himself for it" (Ephesians 5:25), and "Husbands, love your wives [with an affectionate, sympathetic, selfless love that always seeks the best for them] and do not be embittered or resentful toward them [because of the responsibilities of marriage]" (Colossians 3:19 AMP). These precepts Spurgeon epitomized in his marriage to Susannah throughout their 36 years of marriage. "From the beginning, their spiritual love was the bond that strengthened their earthly love."[102] In *John Ploughman's Talk* he wrote: "He who respects his wife will find that she respects him. With what measure he metes it shall be measured to him again, good measure, pressed down, and running over. He who consults his wife will have a good counsellor."[103]

Despite Charles' busy schedule, he didn't neglect Susannah ("wifey" or "Susie" as he called her) or their twin sons. Specifically, each Wednesday (his sabbath day of rest) he spent time alone with her and them at their home. When separated because of ministry obligations (her sickness prevented travel after the first ten years of marriage), Charles would write to her daily. He included her in his ministry. He would ask her counsel on sermonic texts and have her read aloud texts from which he was to preach and reference works dealing with them to help him better understand their flow. He encouraged her to pursue her own writing (she was a masterful author) and the Book Fund ministry. Over the years it distributed 200,000 of mostly his books to 25,000 impoverished pastors. He was her best cheerleader.

In a letter (1871) to Susannah, Charles describes his thankfulness for her: "My Own Dear One—None know how grateful I am to God for you. In all I have ever done for Him, you have a large share, for in making me so happy you have fitted me for service. Not an ounce of power has ever been lost to the good cause through you. I have served the Lord far more, and never less, for your sweet companionship. The Lord God Almighty bless you now and forever!" James T. Allen, in his biography of Spurgeon, wrote, "Mr. Spurgeon's home life was ideal. No one could be an hour under his roof without perceiving the fragrance of domestic affection that pervaded the home. To his invalid wife, he always spoke with a mingled gaiety and affection that was very touching."[104]

A demonstration of that love was exhibited in the construction of their new Helensburgh House (1869). A very small room fit for Susie's use was built by the side of his study. Of that space his biographer wrote, "And nothing had been forgotten which could in any way conduce to the comfort of an invalid almost entirely confined to her couch. He had thought of all things that might please, and there were such tender touches of devoted love upon all the surroundings of the little room that no words can describe her emotions when first she gazed upon them."[105] His love for her was revealed in letters while he was away on ministry: "I must not write more; indeed, matter runs short, except the old, old story of a love which grieves over you and would fain work a miracle and raise you up to perfect health. Yours to love in life, death, and eternally, C. H. S."[106]

And in poems, he was quite a romantic.

Over the space which parts us, my wife,
I'll cast me a bridge of song.
Our hearts shall meet,
O joy of my life, on its arch, unseen, but strong.[107]

~ C. H. S.

Let the husband love his wife as he loves himself, and a little better, for she is his better half. He should feel, *If there's only one good wife in the whole world, I've got her.*

C. H. Spurgeon

His love for Susie exceeded the bounds of his life. He wrote to her, saying, "Remember, all I buy, I pay for. I have paid for everything as yet with the earnings of my pen. *It is my ambition to leave nothing for you to be anxious about.* C. H. S."[108] Her comfort and care, not only during his lifetime, but afterward was of immense importance, and thus planned for ardently.

Spurgeon's family occupied the Helensburgh House, Clapham from 1857–1880, with the rebuilding occurring in 1869. In 1880, Spurgeon's doctor, due to health reasons, advised him to move to higher ground above the smog and damps.[109] Thus Susie and he moved to Westwood, Norwood. Of the move, Spurgeon said, "I did not arrange it myself; the Lord just put a spade underneath me and transplanted me to Norwood."[110]

Here is why he made that assertion. At the first, he dismissed the notion that he could purchase such a grandios property and resolved to pursue it no further. However, shortly afterward, the agents for the property notified him the house still had not been sold and inquired if he yet might be interested. That very day his neighbor offered to buy the Helensburgh home at a price that would enable him to buy the new house.[111] And he did.

Of their new home, Susannah wrote in June 1884: "From the breezy heights of Beulah Hill we command a lovely and uninterrupted view, not of the fair earth merely, but of the fairer firmament above it; our windows are observatories whence many a longing, loving glance is cast heavenwards, and one of the chief pleasures of restful or contemplative hours is found in silently watching the ever-changing aspect of the sky, and noting the manifold glories of that wonderful cloud-land which divides our earthly home from the promised inheritance on high."[112] While the former home remains in existence (now known as Queen Elizabeth House - SW12 8LZ), of the latter no trace remains.

Spurgeon gave his secret of raising godly children. He wrote, "The great secret lies in a large measure in powerful supplication."[113] Spurgeon taught his twin sons to love the Bible and study confessions of faith like the Westminster Catechism and the Second London Confession of 1689. On September 14, 1874, Thomas and Charles were presented to the church for membership and upon sharing the work of grace in their souls were accepted upon the condition of baptism. On Sunday evening, September 21 (a day after their eighteenth birthday), their father baptized them at the Tabernacle.[114]

Charles, Jr., and Thomas followed in their dad's steps, becoming ministers. After their father's death, Thomas became pastor of the Metropolitan Tabernacle (after a brief ministry of A. T. Pierson, October 21, 1891–June 7, 1892), and Charles, Jr., assumed responsibilities of the orphanage his dad founded.[115] Charles, Jr., paid tribute to his father: "If ever a man was sent from God, my father was—a true apostle and a faithful ambassador of Jesus Christ. There was no one who could preach like my father. His humility, his blameless example, his holy consistency, his genial love, his generous liberality, his wise counsel, and his fearless fidelity to God and His truth are all on a par with his faithfulness."[116]

The best testimony of a man's devotion to his wife comes from her. Reflecting upon their marriage, she said they were "two pilgrims treading this highway of life together, hand in hand, heart linked to heart."[117] Susie spent with Charles what came to be his last three months on earth in Mentone, France, a time they both described as "their honeymoon over again." Later Susie spoke of those months as "perfect earthly happiness."[118] The reading of her memoirs of Charles speaks of a lifelong romance and ministry they shared filled with no regrets. (It is almost impossible to lay aside.) With regard to letters he wrote to her, she said, "To the end of his beautiful life it was the same: his letters were always those of a devoted lover, as well as of a tender husband; not only did the brook never dry up, but the stream grew deeper and broader, and the rhythm of its song waxed sweeter and stronger."[119]

In an 1886 memorandum, Susannah wrote, "Oh, blessed wedded love that has grown brighter and clearer after shining on for thirty happy years! Thanks be to God for a love that 'Fonder grows with age, and charms, and charms forever.'"[120] Upon Charles' death, Susannah wrote, "For although God has seen fit to call my beloved up to higher service, He has left me the consolation of still loving him with all my heart and believing that our love shall be perfected when we meet in that blessed land where Love reigns supreme and eternal."[121] On October 22, 1903, she joined her beloved husband in the land "where congregations ne'er break up, and Sabbaths have no end."[122]

Spurgeon's remarks in a *Morning and Evening* entry are a most fitting charge to ministers. He writes, "A husband should love his wife with a constant love, for thus Jesus loves his church. He does not vary in His affection. He may change in His display of affection, but the affection itself is still the same. A husband should love his wife with an enduring love, for nothing 'shall be able to separate us from the love of God, which is in Christ Jesus our Lord' (Romans 8.39). A true husband loves his wife with a hearty love, fervent and intense. It is not mere lip-service."[123]

What saith Spurgeon? Love your wife as Christ loves the church. Sacrifice for your wife as Christ sacrificed for the church. Display love to and for your wife as Christ does for the church. Don't sacrifice your wife (and family) on the altar of ministry. Keep the home fires burning intensely as you fulfill the call of God. And this Spurgeon did with regard to Susannah, until his death on January 31, 1892. To the aspiring pastors at the Pastor's College, he said, "We ought to be such husbands that every husband in the parish [church] may safely be such as we are. Is it so? We ought to be the best of fathers. Alas! some ministers, to my knowledge, are far from this, for as to their families, they have kept the vineyards of others, but their own vineyards they have not kept."[124]

In the sermon "The King and His Court," Spurgeon states, "There is a great deal in the way in which a man walks in his house. It will not do to be a saint abroad and a devil at home! There are some of that kind. They are wonderfully sweet at a prayer meeting, but they are dreadfully sour to their wives and children. This will never do! Every genuine believer should say, and mean it, 'I will walk within my house with a perfect heart.' It is in the home that we get the truest proof of godliness. 'What sort of a man is he?' said one to George Whitefield; and Whitefield answered, 'I cannot say, for I never lived with him.' That is the way to test a man—to live with him."[125]

Paul has an appropriate question for the minister: "If a man knows not how to rule his own house, how shall he take care of the church of God?" (1 Timothy 3:5 KJV2000). Spurgeon well knew how to take care of the former, and therefore was able to aptly by grace care for the latter.

8
Reliance upon the Spirit

"Oh, it were far better to break stones on the road than to be a preacher, unless one had God's Holy Spirit to sustain him; for our charge is solemn and our burden is heavy."[126]

~ C. H. Spurgeon

> Principle: The role the preacher allows the Holy Spirit to play in his ministry determines its extent, effectiveness and endurance.

Paul testified, "I relied only on the power of the Holy Spirit" (1 Corinthians 2:4 NLT), and, "For our Gospel came unto you not in word only, but also in power and in the Holy Ghost" (1 Thessalonians 1:5 KJV21). See 1 Corinthians 2:5. His endurance with adversity in ministry he credits to the Holy Spirit (Acts 20:22; Acts 21:4; Acts 23:11; Galatians 5:16).

And Spurgeon states, "To us, as ministers, the Holy Spirit is absolutely essential. Without Him our office is a mere name. If we have not the Spirit which Jesus promised, we cannot perform the commission which Jesus gave."[127] "Our hope of success, and our strength for continuing service, lie in our belief that the Spirit of the Lord resteth upon us" [Zechariah 4:6].[128] Further, he said, "The lack of distinctly recognizing the power of the Holy Ghost lies at the root of many useless ministries."[129]

In the sermon "Preach the Gospel," Spurgeon recounts a time in his early years preaching in Scotland when "the chariot wheels were taken off; and that the chariot dragged very heavily along."[130] It was a bitterly humbling experience, about which he said, "I would have hidden myself in any obscure corner of the earth. I felt as if I should speak no more in the name of the Lord." (Every minister has been there!) The experience taught him that ministry apart from the infusion of power by the Holy Spirit was powerless and fruitless.

> *Without the Spirit of God, we can do nothing. We are as ships without wind or chariots without steeds. Like branches without sap, we are withered. Like coals without fire, we are useless. As an offering without the sacrificial flame, we are unaccepted.*
> *C. H. Spurgeon*

In the sermon "A Revival of Promise," he frankly states, "Without the Spirit of God, we can do nothing. We are as ships without wind or chariots without steeds. Like branches without sap, we are withered. Like coals without fire, we are useless. As an offering without the sacrificial flame, we are unaccepted. I desire both to feel and to confess this fact whenever I attempt to preach. I do not wish to get away from it, or to conceal it, nor can I, for I am often made to feel it to the deep humbling of my spirit."[131]

In another sermon he said, "The power that is in the Gospel does not lie in the eloquence of the preacher, otherwise men would be converters of souls. Nor does it lie in the preacher's learning, otherwise it could consist of the wisdom of men. We might preach till our tongues rotted, till we should exhaust our lungs and die, but never a soul would be converted unless there were mysterious power going with it. O Sirs! We might as well preach to stone walls as preach to humanity unless the Holy Ghost be with the Word, to give it power to convert the soul."[132]

Ian Murray, biographer of Spurgeon's life, said: "The true explanation of Spurgeon's ministry is to be found in the person and power of the Holy Spirit. He was himself deeply conscious of this."[133]

David Livingstone, missionary and friend to Spurgeon, once asked him, "How do you manage to do two men's work in a single day?"

Spurgeon replied, "You have forgotten that there are two of us."[134] (The Holy Spirit and Spurgeon).

Spurgeon's deep reliance upon the Holy Spirit in preaching was said (though undocumented) to be manifest each time he ascended the double spiral staircase to the higher level where the pulpit was located at the Metropolitan Tabernacle saying softly to himself at each step (each stairwell consisted of fifteen steps), "I believe in the Holy Spirit. I believe in the Holy Spirit."[135] Fifteen times he would reinforce his trust in and dependence upon the Holy Spirit to anoint the sermon and himself.

In *An All-Round Ministry* Spurgeon states, "In this grand, yet delicate labor [ministry], *we have to persevere year after year*. What power can enable us to do this? While so many complain of the monotony of the old Gospel and feel a perpetual itching for something new, this disease may even infect our own hearts. When we feel dull and stale, we must not imagine that the truth of God is so; nay, rather, by returning more closely to the Word of the Lord, we must renew our freshness. To continue always steadfast in the faith, so that our latest testimony shall be identical in substance with our first testimony, only deeper, mellower, more assured, and more intense—this is such a labor that for it we must have the power of God."[136]

And then he pleads, "Wherefore should we undertake what we have not the power to perform? Supernatural work needs supernatural power, and if you have it not, do not attempt to do the work alone. This supernatural force is the power of the Holy Ghost, the power of Jehovah Himself."[137] And in *Lectures to My Students* he drives the point further home: "It is extraordinary power from God, not talent, that wins the day. It is extraordinary spiritual unction, not extraordinary mental power, that we need. Mental power may fill a chapel, but spiritual power fills the church with soul anguish. Mental power may gather a large congregation, but only spiritual power will save souls. What we need is spiritual power."[138]

Spurgeon says in the sermon "My Prayer," "The prayer before us, 'Quicken Thou me in Thy way,' deals with the believer's frequent need. You yourselves know, in your own souls, that your spirit is most apt to become sluggish and that you have need frequently to put up this prayer, 'Quicken Thou me.' If there is a prayer in the book which well becomes my lips, it is just this."[139] Why? Saith Spurgeon, "All the hope of our ministry lies in the Spirit of God operating on the spirits of men."[140]

"The Holy Spirit is absolutely needful," he says, "to make everything that we do to be alive. The preacher must preach living truth in a living manner if he expects to obtain a hundred-fold harvest. How much there is of church work which is nothing better than the movement of a galvanized corpse. How much of religion is done as if it were performed by machinery. *We can preach as machines, we can pray as machines, and we can teach Sunday school as machines.* Yes, and we ourselves shall do so unless the Spirit of God be with us. Most hearers know what it is to hear a live sermon which quivers all over with fulness of energy; you also know what it is to sing a hymn in a lively manner, and you know what it is to unite in a live prayer-meeting; but, ah, if the Spirit of God be absent, all that the church does will be lifeless, the rustle of leaves above a tomb."[141]

In the sermon "The Holy Spirit's Chief Office," he states, "We, my brethren, who are preachers of the Word, have but a short time to live; let us dedicate all that time to the glorious work of magnifying Christ." How? He continues, "If we alone had the task of glorifying Christ, we might be beaten; but as the Holy Spirit is the Glorifier of Christ, His glory is in very safe hands."[142]

9
Feed the Flame

"Go to the heavenly hills and gather fuel there; pile on the glorious logs of the wood of Lebanon, and the fire will burn freely and yield a sweet perfume as each piece of choice cedar glows in the flame."[143]

~ C. H. Spurgeon

> Principle. Feed the flame of others but not to the neglect of fueling your own fire.

The Shunamite woman (Song of Solomon 1:6) was entrusted with the care of the vineyards of others, which she managed well, howbeit, at the neglect of her own. She testifies, "They made me the keeper of the vineyards; but mine own vineyard have I not kept" (Song of Solomon 1:6). She enabled the vineyards of others to stay pruned and thus bear much fruit, while her own was overtaken with weeds and thorns, yielding little or no fruit.

Regrettably, her fault is the fault of many in the ministry. While busily caring for the spiritual welfare of others, they are negligent of the work needed in their own vineyard. They promote the growth of others spiritually, while they remain stunted. They fuel the fire of others, while their own fire, perhaps unknown to them, dies out.

In the sermon "He Blessed Him There," Spurgeon states, "We miss a thousand blessings because we are too busy to commune with God. We are here, there, and everywhere, except where we ought to be."[144] "It will be in vain for me to stock my library," he says to the preacher, "or organize societies, or project schemes, if I neglect the culture of myself; for books and agencies and systems are only remotely the instruments of my holy calling. My own spirit, soul, and body are my nearest machinery for sacred service; my spiritual faculties and my inner life are my battle axe and weapons of war. For the herald of the Gospel to be spiritually out of order in his own proper person is, both to himself and to his work, a most serious calamity."[145]

"The fire on the altar must be kept burning; it must never go out. Each morning the priest will add fresh wood to the fire and arrange the burnt offering on it....Remember, the fire must be kept burning on the altar at all times. It must never go out" (Leviticus 6:12–13 NLT). The minister, spiritually, is to keep the fire upon his heart's altar burning continuously, lest he become stale, complacent, discouraged, impotent, and fainthearted. Ignite the heart furnace to full pitch and then 'every morning add fresh wood to the fire' (the study of Holy Scripture, meditation, communion with the Lord, unfeigned repentance) so that it will burn steadily with intense heat, not in flutters. Aim at being like fixed stars that shine with a constant light consistently, rather than like comets that appear with a mighty blaze only soon to disappear. Having received the fire supernaturally, the preacher is responsible for maintaining it (keep the "fire" alive) through the enablement of the Holy Spirit.

What is said on Sunday, to be most impactful, must "pass through the fire of an intense spiritual life in the preacher."[146] "The fire on the altar must be kept burning; it must never go out." Otherwise, he will preach amidst gray ashes with little power and vitality, and slumber in the work. May the motto on the preacher's banner and fervent prayer of his heart be that of David Brainerd: "Oh, that I were a flaming fire in the service of my God."[147]

Jesus said of John the Baptist, "He was a burning and a shining light" (John 5:35). "Blessed eulogy! may it be earned by each one of us. 'Burning and shining'—our very ideal of a minister; a hot heart with a clear head; impetuosity and prudence blended; zeal and knowledge linked in holy wedlock."[148] Amen and amen. Let's keep fanning the flame. New manna is to be gathered 'fresh' every morning (Exodus 16:21).

Paul continually fed and fanned the flame in his soul. He said, "I die daily" (1 Corinthians 15:31). "This one thing I do....I press toward the mark [goal] for the prize of the high calling of God" (Philippians 3:13–14). "Present your bodies a living sacrifice, holy, acceptable unto God, which is your reasonable service" (Romans 12:1). "I discipline my body and keep it under control, lest after preaching to others I myself should be disqualified" (1 Corinthians 9:27 ESV).

And Spurgeon practiced the same. "Old anointings will not suffice," says Spurgeon, "to impart unction to thy spirit; thine head must have fresh oil poured upon it from the golden horn of the sanctuary, or it will cease from its glory."[149] Spurgeon daily met with God, before he met with any man.

10
Approval of God, Not Man

"To you comes the divine command, and it is for you to obey it, whether you are advised by others to do so or not. Even to ask for such advice is to trifle with the authority of God."[150]

~ C. H. Spurgeon

> **Principle:**
> Preach to
> please God, not
> for the flattery,
> amusement,
> and approval of
> man.

Paul had received his commission to preach straight from God and didn't 'confer with flesh and blood' to get approval (Galatians 1:16).

Spurgeon observes, "I have generally found that when men do consult with flesh and blood, the consultation usually leads to the neglect of duty and the forsaking of the Lord. Had Paul conferred with flesh and blood, he would probably never have been an apostle. I pray that you, beloved, may have the grace to say, 'My Master's command is my only law.' My Master tells me to do such and such; this is my excuse if men say that I play the fool by doing it, if they charge me with throwing prudence to the winds, and even if they thrust me into prison and lead me out to die. Sooner let the sun refuse to shine at the Almighty's bidding, sooner let the earth refuse to revolve on her axis or any longer to traverse her orbit, sooner let all nature revolt against the laws of its Maker than a man of God, redeemed by the blood of Christ, should ever dare to refuse to obey Him, let Him command whatever He may."[151]

Knowledge of one's call and commission negates the need to confer with a man about whether or not it is valid or should be pursued. Not conferring with flesh and blood (seeking man's approval or affirmation) connects with Paul's assertion that he didn't seek to please any man in ministry, but only the Lord. "So we speak [and minister]; not as pleasing men, but God" (1 Thessalonians 2:4).

A young violinist, when ending his first concert, was applauded by a standing audience. Amidst the approval of the crowd, his eyes stayed fixed the entire time upon an elderly man seated in the balcony. The young violinist showed no emotion of joy until that man stood and applauded. You see, that elderly man was the young violinist's instructor, and he was only concerned with pleasing him.

Such was the attitude of Paul with regard to Christ, for he testifies, "Obviously, I'm not trying to win the approval of people, but of God. If pleasing people were my goal, I would not be Christ's servant" (Galatians 1:10 NLT), and, "Our purpose is to please God, not people" (1 Thessalonians 2:4 NLT). John MacArthur remarks, "Paul was far more concerned with obeying his divine calling than with gaining man's approval. Only one thing mattered—pleasing the Master."[152]

F. F. Bruce states, "Pleasing men and women was not what Paul was called to do. He was called to serve Christ; he could not make that his business and aim to please his hearers at the same time."[153]

The same goes for every minister. Preach and serve to please an audience of ONE. It's God's approval, not that of the church or its leaders, that ultimately matters and counts (Romans 14:12). Saith Spurgeon, "Long ago I ceased to count heads. Truth is usually in the minority in this evil world. I have faith in the Lord Jesus for myself, a faith burned into me as with a hot iron. I thank God, what I believe I shall believe, even if I believe it alone."[154]

Paul Chappell says, "Fear of man is the enemy of the fear of the Lord. The fear of man pushes us to perform for man's approval rather than according to God's directives."[155] See Proverbs 29:25.

Saith Spurgeon, "The minister who cares for any man's opinion when he is doing his duty is unworthy of his office. The servant of God must not be the servant of men. The only man whom God will bless is he who fears no man's face and resolves that whether he offends or pleases he will clear his soul from the blood of all men."[156]

Spurgeon practiced what he preached. He, like John Knox (who opposed Catholic Mary, Queen of Scots), feared the face of no man (Jeremiah 1:8). During the Down-Grade Controversy (1887–1888) his stance against theological biblical liberalism in the Baptist Union went against the tide and cost him dearly. Susannah attested that the spiritual warfare took ten years off his life. When one seeks to please God rather than man, suffering is often the consequence. See 2 Timothy 2:3.

> Fearless myself, a dying man,
> Of dying man's esteem,
> I preach as though I ne'er might preach again,
> A dying man to dying men.[157]

John Stott states, "Although we have responsibilities to others, we are primarily accountable to God. It is before Him that we stand, and to Him that one day we must give an account. We should not therefore rate human opinion too highly, becoming depressed when criticized and elated when flattered."[158] George McDonald states, "When one has learned to seek the honor that cometh from God only, he will take the withholding of the honor that cometh by man very lightly indeed."[159]

11
Retreat, Rest, and Renewal
"It is wisdom to take occasional furlough."[160]

~ C. H. Spurgeon

Principle: "Come apart" or fall apart.

The earnest pastor is like the Dunkin' Donut man in the television commercial who meets himself at the door to his home saying, "Am I going or coming?" Jesus taught the need for overtaxed, worn-out preachers to have time for renewal and relaxation by a change of scenery and a break from ministerial labor. He said, "Come with me by yourselves to a place where we can be alone, and you can get some rest" (Mark 6:31 CJB).

Vance Havner remarked, "Jesus knows we must come apart and rest awhile, or else we may just plain come apart." Saith Hudson Taylor, "To every toiling, heavy-laden sinner, Jesus says, 'Come to Me and rest.' But there are many toiling, heavy-laden believers, too. For them this same invitation is meant. Note well the word of Jesus, if you are heavy-laden with your service, and do not mistake it. It is not, 'Go; labor on,' as perhaps you imagine. On the contrary, it is stop; turn back; 'Come to Me and rest.' Never, never did Christ send a heavy-laden one to work; never, never did He send a hungry one, a weary one, a sick or sorrowing one away on any service. For such the Bible only says, 'Come; come; come.'"[161]

Ministerial labor produces times of exhaustion mentally and physically. David fainted in battle (2 Samuel 21:15), Elijah became overwrought and worn out (1 Kings 19:4–8), Moses grew exhausted in intercession (Exodus 17:12), the disciples became overtaxed meeting the demands of the multitudes (Mark 6:31), and Paul knew weariness and painfulness from long days of ministry that were coupled with sleepless nights (2 Corinthians 11:27). God's servants require "a breathing space in a life of toil."[162]

Spurgeon says, "The bow cannot be always bent without the fear of breaking. Repose is as needful to the mind as sleep to the body. Our Sabbaths are our days of toil, and if we do not rest upon some other day, we shall break down. Even the earth must lie fallow and have her Sabbaths, and so must we. Hence the wisdom and compassion of our Lord when he said to his disciples, 'Let us go into the desert and rest awhile.'[163]

Mike Yaconelli wrote, "Rest is listening to our weariness and responding to our tiredness. Rest is what happens when we say one simple word: 'No!' Rest is the ultimate humiliation, because in order to rest, we must admit we are not necessary, that the world can get along without us, that God's work does not depend on us. Once we understand how unnecessary we are, only then might we find the right reasons to say yes. Only then might we find the right reasons to decide to *be with* Jesus instead of *working for* him."[164]

Scripture is silent about Paul's rest times, but it appears that he took time off in Antioch between his second and third missionary journeys (Acts 18:23). John MacArthur suggests "possibly from the summer of A.D. 52 to the spring of A.D 53)."[165] And though not ideal, the approximate five years he spent in custody—about two and a half years spent in a literal jail cell, the rest spent under house arrest or under escort by a Roman guard to Rome—provided a break from the grueling and taxing schedule. Paul did observe the Sabbath, the first day of the week (Acts 18:4), though it was mingled with "work" as it is with present-day pastors.

> *While we are in this tabernacle, we must every now and then cry halt and serve the Lord by holy inaction and consecrated leisure.*
> *C. H. Spurgeon*

Spurgeon encouraged ministers to frequently retreat from ministerial work: "Rest time is not waste time. In the long run, we shall do more by sometimes doing less. On, on, on forever, without recreation, may suit spirits emancipated from this 'heavy clay,' but while we are in this tabernacle, we must every now and then cry halt and serve the Lord by holy inaction and consecrated leisure. Let no tender conscience doubt the lawfulness of going out of harness for a while, but learn from the experience of others the necessity and duty of taking timely rest."[166] "A day's breathing of fresh air upon the hills," writes Spurgeon, "or a few hours 'ramble in the woods' umbrageous [shady] calm,' would sweep the cobwebs out of the brain of scores of our toiling ministers who are now but half alive!"[167] In lecturing the students at the Pastor's College, he cautioned them not to be negligent of their bodies. Using Lucan's words, he implored, "See thou twist not the rope so hard that it break."[168]

Spurgeon certainly twisted the rope to its breaking point, often working 18 hours a day six days a week.[169] He ministered without a holiday from 1854–1860.[170] He told preachers, "Crowd as much as you can into every day, and postpone no work till tomorrow,"[171] which he practiced. But with the strenuous labor, he realized the need for renewal and rest, so he took retreats (vacations) to Scotland (two weeks each summer) and Mentone, France (a month or six weeks each winter), [172] which in all probability prolonged his life and ministry.[173]

Writing of the benefit of a time of rest in Mentone, he says, "I do not think any human being upon earth ever felt so much repose of soul and body as I do. Many years of toil are all rewarded by this blessed rest, which only seems too good to be true. The burden is taken from the shoulder, and the bit from between the jaws. If anything can make me feel young and strong again, this will."[174] Spurgeon speaks of fishing in Mentone.[175] And he "kept, when possible, Wednesday as his day of rest."[176] However, "Spurgeon never took a vacation from his vocation."[177]

His garden was also a source of relaxation and pleasure, of which he said, "My Master, I am sure, does not grudge me the enjoyment of my garden. I owe it to Him. It is about the only luxury in which I indulge. I am very hard worked. I have no social intercourse on account of the limited time at my disposal. I have neither time nor strength to move about and find refreshment in variety and change as others do; but I have my garden, with its flowers and its fine prospects, and I praise Him for it."[178] And Spurgeon found delight and rest in taking walks in the countryside.

Talmage wrote, "Luther used to sport with his children; Edmund Burke used to caress his favorite horse; Thomas Chalmers, in the dark hour of the Church's disruption, played kite for recreation, and the busy Christ said to the busy apostles, 'Come ye apart awhile into the desert and rest yourselves.' And I have observed that they who do not know how to rest do not know how to work."[179]

H. J. Wilmot-Buxton says, "On our journey from earth to Heaven, we need some quiet harbors, some peaceful spots where we can find rest. Jesus has built such cities of refuge for us, His pilgrims, and provided quiet havens for His people as they pass over the waves of this troublesome world."[180] For Spurgeon, these havens were Mentone in Southern France (Hotel Beau Rivage) and Scotland (Benmore), but primarily the former.

Work hard and "crowd as much as you can into every day, and postpone no work till tomorrow," as Spurgeon implored, but don't neglect periods of rest and recreation in the process. Find a Mentone or Benmore to frequent regularly for refreshment and renewal. Times of rest will build stamina and strength for continuance in and betterment of ministry. Churches ought to encourage vacations, retreats, or sabbaticals for their pastor, and Metropolitan Tabernacle did. On December 26, 1878, the deacons at Spurgeon's church wrote a letter to him urging a three-month sabbatical.[181]

12

A Fixed Focus

"Turn all the springs of your soul into one channel, causing it to flow onward in an undivided stream."[182]

~ C. H. Spurgeon

> **Principle:** Focusing on Jesus in the storm, as Peter did, keeps the preacher from sinking.

The author of Hebrews says, "Consider him that endured such contradiction of sinners against himself, lest ye be wearied and faint in your minds" (Hebrews 12:3). Paul withstood the trials of ministry because of a concentrated gaze upon Jesus (Philippians 1:21). He exhorted, "Set your mind on things above, not on things on the earth" (Colossians 3:2 NKJV).

It's when the minister's primary focus shifts from the worship of Him to the working for Him that he, like Peter on the tumultuous water, begins to sink. "This one thing I do" (Philippians 3:13). Isaiah testifies of the persevering power of a fixed focus on the Lord: "You will guard him and keep him in perfect and constant peace whose mind [both its inclination and its character] is stayed on You, because he commits himself to You, leans on You, and hopes confidently in You" (Isaiah 26:2 AMPC).

Spurgeon, in the sermon "The Rule of the Race," emphasizes the need of soul focus on Jesus in the Christian's race (walk, work, ministry). He states, "The Greek word for 'looking' is a much fuller word than we can find in the English language. It has a preposition in it which turns the look away from everything else. You are to look from all beside to Jesus. Fix not your gaze upon the cloud of witnesses; they will hinder you if they take away your eyes from Jesus. Look not on the weights and the besetting sin—these you have laid aside; look away from them. Do not even look upon the racecourse or the competitors, but look to Jesus and so start in the race. What have you to trust to but His blood and righteousness? Beware that you set up nothing as a rival confidence. Look off from everything you have ever relied upon in days gone by, and say to your soul, 'None but Jesus.' You must have a single eye and a single hope. 'Christ is all,' and He must be all to you, or you are out of the race altogether."[183]

Albert Barnes remarks, "We will not forget that our reliance is not on armies, but on God, the living God. Whatever instrumentality we may employ, we will remember always that our hope is in God, and that He only can give success."[184] W. S. Plumer writes, "The righteous put nothing with God to form the basis of their joy and trust. He alone is enough. They need neither help, nor guidance, nor wisdom, nor strength, nor righteousness but in Him alone."[185]

I'll trust Thee; oh, I'll trust Thee.
Evermore I'll trust Thee.
I know Thine arms are 'round me,
Wherever I may be,
Wherever I may be.
~ William Henry Gardner (1898)

> Suffer your entire nature to be led in captivity by Jesus Christ, and lay everything at His dear feet who bled and died for you.
> Charles Spurgeon

Oswald Chambers gives caution to the minister: "Beware of any work for God that causes or allows you to avoid concentrating on Him. A great number of Christian workers worship their work. The only concern of Christian workers should be their concentration on God. A worker who lacks this serious controlling emphasis of concentration on God is apt to become overly burdened by his work. Consequently, he *becomes burned out and defeated.* There is no freedom and no delight in life at all. His nerves, mind, and heart are so overwhelmed that God's blessing cannot rest on him."[186] Max Lucado gives great counsel: "Focus on giants—you stumble. Focus on God—giants tumble."[187] Saith Spurgeon: "Suffer your entire nature to be led in captivity by Jesus Christ, and lay everything at His dear feet who bled and died for you."[188]

When a young boy, David Livingstone, a friend of Spurgeon and who spoke at the Tabernacle, was called to the deathbed of a faithful Christian warrior for a word of counsel. He said, "My son, make religion the everyday business of your life, and not a thing of fits and starts."[189] Livingstone heeded that advice, made the cause of Christ the fixed focus of life, and ignited a light in the darkness of Africa that has never been extinguished. Maintain the gospel focus. Keep the main thing, the main thing.

13
The Sword of the Spirit

"It was God's Word that made us; is it any wonder that His Word should sustain us?"[190]

~ C. H. Spurgeon

> Principle: The world, the flesh, and the Devil cannot deter or defeat the preacher that wields the Sword of the Spirit.

The "sword of the Spirit" enabled Paul's effectiveness and endurance in ministry. Of this, his writings at large and reference to the sword of the Spirit specifically bear witness (Ephesians 6:17).

Albert Barnes remarked about Ephesians 6:17, "A single text of Scripture is better to meet a temptation than all the philosophy which the world contains. The tempter can reason, and reason plausibly too. But he cannot resist a direct and positive command of the Almighty. Had Eve adhered simply to the Word of God and urged His command, without attempting to "reason" about it, she would have been safe. The Savior met the tempter with the Word of God, and He was foiled (Matthew 4:4). So we shall be safe if we adhere to the simple declarations of the Bible and oppose a temptation by a positive command of God."[191]

Saith Adam Clarke, "An ability to quote this [Holy Scripture] on proper occasions, and especially in times of temptation and trial, has a wonderful tendency to cut in pieces the snares of the adversary."[192] C. S. Robinson says of the sword of the Spirit, "It will of itself fight, it will of itself conquer, and in the end it will defend and deliver every brave man who trusts it."[193]

Spurgeon's compass and anchor in storms he faced in ministry were the Holy Scriptures. He testified, "For my own part, *I have no shadow of a hope but in the word of the Lord;* his Spirit has delivered me from all reliance upon duties or feelings or experiences. The Word of the Lord is the life of my soul. In the words of King Jesus there is power to save you, to renew you, to pardon you, *to preserve you*, to sanctify you, and to perfect you. If you have hold on the promises, they will hold you for time and eternity too."[194]

Here is the way to be kept steadfast—
"The Word of God abideth in you."
Charles Spurgeon

Again he said, "Here is the way to be kept steadfast—'The Word of God abideth in you.' 'The Word of God'—that is to say, we are to believe in the doctrines of God's Word, and these will make us strong. What vigor they infuse into a man! Get the Word well into you, and you will overcome the wicked one."[195] He continues, "The Word of God will be to you a bulwark and a high tower, a castle of defense against the foe. Oh, see to it that the Word of God is in you, in your very soul, permeating your thoughts."[196] "Within the Scriptures there is a balm for every wound and a salve for every sore!"[197]

Therefore, he counsels, "Lean your whole weight on the Word, and you shall find it to be like Mount Zion, which cannot be removed, but abideth forever."[198]

Lecturing to "preachers" at the Pastor's College he said, "In case the famine of books should be sore in the land, there is one book which you all have, and that is your Bible; and a minister with his Bible is like David with his sling and stone, fully equipped for the fray. No man may say that he has no well to draw from while the Scriptures are within reach. In the Bible we have a perfect library, and he who studies it thoroughly will be a better scholar than if he had devoured the Alexandrian Library entire."[199]

In the sermon "The Last Words of Christ on the Cross," Spurgeon says, "Oh, that you and I might get into the very heart of the Word of God, and get that Word into ourselves! As I have seen the silkworm eat into the leaf and consume it, so ought we to do with the Word of the Lord—not crawl over its surface, but eat right into it till we have taken it into our inmost parts. It is idle merely to let the eye glance over the words or to recollect the poetical expressions or the historic facts, but it is blessed to eat into the very soul of the Bible until, at last, you come to talk in Scriptural language and your very style is fashioned upon Scripture models, and, what is better still, your spirit is flavored with the words of the Lord."[200]

Further, in *Morning and Evening,* he asserts to Christians at large, but especially applicable to pastors, "There are times when solitude is better than society and silence is wiser than speech. We should be better Christians if we were more alone, waiting upon God and gathering through meditation on His Word spiritual strength for labor in his service. We ought to muse upon the things of God, because we thus get the real nutriment out of them. Our souls are not nourished merely by listening awhile to this and then to that and then to the other part of divine truth. Hearing, reading, marking, and learning all require inwardly digesting to complete their usefulness, and the inward digesting of the truth lies for the most part in meditating upon it. Why is it that some Christians, although they hear many sermons, make but slow advances in the divine life? Because they neglect their closets and do not thoughtfully meditate on God's Word. They love the wheat, but they do not grind it; they would have the corn, but they will not go forth into the fields to gather it; the fruit hangs upon the tree, but they will not pluck it; the water flows at their feet, but they will not stoop to drink it. From such folly deliver us, O Lord, and be this our resolve: 'I will meditate in Thy precepts.'"[201]

> I'll trust Thee, blessed Lord,
> Altho' the shadows come;
> Sufficient is Thy word,
> Thou pure and holy One!
>
> ~ William Henry Gardner (1898)

To withstand the assaults of the "evil one," take up the sword of the Spirit. Saith Spurgeon, "Difficulties meet us even in standing our ground, for the apostle two or three times bids us: "Stand" (Ephesians 6:13). In the rush of the fight, men are apt to be carried off their legs. If they can keep their footing, they will be victorious; but if they are borne down by the rush of their adversaries, everything is lost. You are to put on the heavenly armor in order that you may stand, and you will need it to maintain the position in which your Captain has placed you. If even to stand requires all this care, judge ye what the warfare must be! Ours, therefore, is a stern conflict, standing and withstanding; and we shall want all the armor from the divine magazine, all the strength from the mighty God of Jacob. The one note that rings out from the text [Ephesians 6:17] is this:—TAKE THE SWORD! TAKE THE SWORD!"[202]

In the sermon "The Folly of Unbelief," Spurgeon said, "Brethren, a want of familiarity with the Word of God is very often the seed-plot of our doubts! Half our fears arise from neglect of the Bible. Our spirits sink for want of the heavenly food stored up in the inspired Volume."[203]

The giants of despair, doubt, and despondency are driven back by the sword of the Spirit. Grasp it in adversity, as Paul and Spurgeon did, "and find in the grasping that somewhat of the divine power comes unto our arm."[204]

14

Proven Armor

"Let Saul's coat be ever so rich, and his armor ever so strong, what is David the better if they fit him not?"[205]

~ Matthew Henry

> Principle: Don't go to battle clad in another man's armor.

Paul wrote, "By the grace of God I am what I am" (1 Corinthians 15:10). He chose to be who he was rather than trying to be someone else. Grace molds the preacher into God's design to fit him for his divine assignment and provides whatever consolation and help are needed in the pilgrimage to Heaven. Saith Spurgeon, "So you, my brother, you may be the cup, and I will be the basin; but let the cup be a cup, and the basin a basin, and each one of us just what he is fitted to be. Be yourself, dear brother, for, if you are not yourself, you cannot be anybody else; and so, you see, you must be nobody."[206]

Identify your gift. Fixate on it. Don't let adversity cause questioning of it. Operate within its element for greater usefulness to the kingdom, and for your joy (Ephesians 4:7). It is when the minister oversteps the boundary of the "gift" bestowed that frustration develops, productivity is impacted and fainting often occurs.

Spurgeon comments, "We must minister as the Spirit has given us the ability, and not intrude upon our fellow servant's domain. Our Lord taught us not to covet the high places, but to be willing to be the least among the brethren."[207] A square peg, regardless of personal effort or outside pressure from others, cannot fit into a round hole properly and effectively. Saul's armor didn't fit David, nor will another man's armor—mannerism, style, approach, delivery—fit you (1 Samuel 17:39).

J. Vernon McGee states, "What a lesson there is for us in this. Let's not try to be something we are not or try to do something we are really not called to do. If God has called you to use a slingshot, friend, don't try to use a sword. If God has called you to speak, then speak. If God has called you to do something else, well, do that. If God has called you to sing, sing. But if He has not called you to sing, for goodness' sake, don't do it. Too many people are trying to use a sword when the slingshot is really more their size."[208]

Saith Spurgeon, "Friend, be true to your own destiny! One man would make a splendid preacher of downright hard-hitting Saxon; why must he ruin himself by cultivating an ornate style? Another attempting to be extremely simple would throw himself away, for he is florid by nature; why should he not follow his bent? Apollos has the gift of eloquence; why must he copy blunt Cephas? Every man in his own order. It seems to me; that nowadays every man prefers his own disorder. Let each man find out what God wants him to do, and then let him do it or die in the attempt. In what way can I bring my Lord most glory and be of most service to His Church while I am here? Solve that question and pass into the practical."[209]

In *Ploughman's Talk* Spurgeon wrote, "Don't hold back because you cannot preach in St. Paul's; be content to talk to one or two in a cottage. Very good wheat grows in little fields. You may cook in small pots as well as in big ones. Little pigeons can carry great messages. Even a little dog can bark at a thief, wake up the master, and save the house. A spark is fire. A sentence of truth has Heaven in it. Do what you do right thoroughly, pray over it heartily, and leave the result to God."[210]

Alexander Maclaren said, "God's fighters have often been tempted to don Saul's armor, and it has always hampered them. It may have shielded them from some assaults, but it has robbed them of elasticity and half-stifled them. They are stronger far without than with it."[211] Further he writes, there are "no blunders in the equipment with which He supplies us. He does not give me the parcel that was meant for you; there is no error in the delivery. He does not send His soldiers to the North Pole equipped for warfare in Africa. He does not give this man a blessing that the man's circumstances would not require. No, no; blessed be God, He cannot err."[212]

God gives to each who is "called out" the specific ability and gifts required for the assigned task. This Peter expresses in 1 Peter 4:11: "If any man minister, let him do it according to the ability which God giveth, that God in all things may be glorified through Jesus Christ, to whom be praise and dominion forever and ever. Amen." And also, Paul, "But unto every one of us is given grace according to the measure of the gift of Christ" (Ephesians 4:7 KJV21).

James Stewart advises: "Be yourself—forget yourself. God has given to each man his own individuality, and standardization is emphatically no part of the divine intention for your ministry. How intolerably dull it would be if every preacher had to be cut to the same pattern! You are to give free rein to your personality....Be yourself. And do not complain if you cannot be someone else...but also forget yourself. You are to use for the delivery of the Word every faculty God has given you, and simultaneously you are to renounce yourself utterly, so that in the end the messenger shall be nothing, the message everything. You are not to cramp or stifle your individuality, but you are to offer it so completely to God upon the altar that when the service closes, the dominating thought in the worshippers' minds will be not of any obtrusive human proficiency or cleverness, but only this: 'The Lord was in His holy temple today!'"[213]

J. Eadie said, "The amount and character of 'grace' possessed by others ought surely to create *no uneasiness nor jealousy*, for it is of Christ's measurement as well as of His bestowment, and every form and quantity of it as it descends from the one source is indispensable to the harmony of the Church."[214] Another said, "Grace is not given in equal measures as the manna in the wilderness; Christ, as the great Bestower, measures out His gifts, and each receives according to His measure. Compare the parable of talents. These are varied, because what each gets, he gets for the good of the rest."[215]

Augustine said, "A wooden key is not so beautiful as a golden one, but if it can open the door when the golden one cannot, it is far more useful."[216] God uses "wooden keys" to do that which "golden keys" cannot. Jon Courson says, "In the body of Christ, each part functions in a unique way according to the gift each has been given."[217] It is only when the believer functions accordingly (employs his divinely designed armor) that the church and kingdom is the most benefited and they are the most effective. Note, as you cannot wear another's armor (effectively), don't pressure others to wear yours. Don't judge or gauge as inferior another minister's armor simply because it differs from yours. And conversely, don't belittle your armor because it doesn't measure up to another's.

"Raw recruits" (as Spurgeon called them) have no shortage of veteran preachers who offer them their armor. May they refuse it, as David did Saul's. To them I say, be you, not the caricature of another, in ministry. Advises Spurgeon,

"Gifts differ—be natural! Be yourself. Some people say, 'What a lovely tree.' I say, 'What a horribly ugly thing it is.' Why not let the tree grow as God would have it. Do not clip yourselves round or square, but keep your freshness."[218] Be whom God intended! Don't be squeezed into the "mold" of another's making. Stay with the armor that fits YOU. If the armor you wear doesn't fit, brazenly change it for that which does.

15

Preaching Christ and the Cross

"The sermon which does not lead to Christ, or of which Jesus Christ is not the top and the bottom, is a sort of sermon that will make the devils in hell laugh, but might make the angels of God weep."[219]

~ C. H. Spurgeon

> Principle: The degree to which the minister tethers himself and his work to the Cross determines his success.

Paul and Spurgeon never drifted from the centrality of the Cross in their preaching and ministry. Paul brazenly said, "For I determined [decided] not to know anything among you, save Jesus Christ, and Him crucified" (1 Corinthians 2:2), and, "For though I preach the gospel, I have nothing to glory of: for necessity is laid upon me; yea, woe is unto me, if I preach not the gospel" (1 Corinthians 9:16). Paul's mission was not to baptize (1 Corinthians 1:17), not to preach self (2 Corinthians 4:5), not to parade magnificent speech or teach philosophy (1 Corinthians 2:1 AMP), but to everyone preach "Christ, and Him crucified."

Saith Spurgeon: "As to the matter of preaching the Gospel, Paul was always ready for that; he kept not back any one of its truths, nor any part of its teaching. Even if it should bring upon him ridicule and contempt, though it should be to the Jews a stumbling block and to the Greeks foolishness, Paul would say, 'As much as in me is, I am ready to preach the gospel' to them all."[220]

Oswald Chambers declared, "The apostle Paul had a strong and steady underlying consistency in his life. Consequently, he could let his external life change without internal distress because he was rooted and grounded in God. The great basis of his consistency was the agony of God in the redemption of the world, namely, the Cross of Christ."[221]

And Spurgeon testified to the same. "I wish that our ministry—that mine especially—might be tied and tethered to the Cross. I would have no other subject to set before you but Jesus only."[222] He remarked, "To preach Jesus and to win souls, and not to gain money or human applause, must be the way in which you prove that you glory in the Cross. What shall I say to young men who are about to enter the ministry that shall be more useful to them than this? Keep to the Cross; keep to the Cross! Always preach up Jesus Christ! Always preach up Jesus Christ! I think no sermon should be without the doctrine of salvation by faith in it."[223]

No Christ in your sermon, sir? Then go home, and never preach again until you have something worth preaching.
Charles Spurgeon

In "Saving Souls Our One Business," he instructs, "Give the people every truth baptized in holy fire, and each truth will have its own useful effect upon the mind. But the great truth is the Cross, the truth that 'God so loved the world.'...Beloved, keep to that. That is the bell for you to ring. Ring it and keep on ringing it."[224] Frankly he said, "No Christ in your sermon, sir? Then go home, and never preach again until you have something worth preaching."[225]

Spurgeon's practice was to take a text and make a beeline to the Cross.[226] In the sermon "Christ Precious to Believers," he quotes a Welsh preacher who emphasizes this aim in preaching. "I have never yet found a text that had not got a road to Christ in it, and if I ever do find one that has not a road to Christ in it, I will make one; I will go over hedge and ditch but I would get at my Master, for the sermon cannot do any good unless there is a savor of Christ in it."[227]

Saith Spurgeon to every minister: "We must throw all our strength of judgment, memory, imagination, and eloquence into the delivery of the Gospel and not give to the preaching of the Cross our random thoughts while wayside topics engross our deeper meditations. Brethren, first and above all things, keep to plain evangelical doctrines; whatever else you do or do not preach, be sure incessantly to bring forth the soul-saving truth of Christ and him crucified."[228] Saith William A. Quayle, "The tongue's holiest mission is to proclaim the Christ."[229]

The chief surgeon at a hospital in Paris asked Dr. Astley Cooper, an English surgeon visiting the city, the number of times he had performed a certain operation. He replied that he had performed it thirteen times. "Ah, but, monsieur," the French surgeon responded, "I have done it one hundred and sixty times."

He then asked the English doctor how many of the thirteen people on which he performed the surgery lived. With a look of blank amazement on Cooper's face, he replied, "I saved eleven out of the thirteen. How many did you save out of one hundred and sixty?"

The French surgeon replied, "Ah, monsieur, I loss dem all; but de operation was very brilliant."

In relating that story, Spurgeon made this application: "Of how many popular ministries might the same verdict be given! Souls are not saved, but the preaching is very brilliant. Thousands are attracted and operated on by the rhetorician's art, but what if he should have to say of his admirers, 'I lost them all, but the sermons were very brilliant!'"[230]

In the sermon "Preach the Gospel," Spurgeon says, "Calvary preaching, Calvary theology, Calvary books, Calvary sermons! These are the things we want. And in proportion as we have Calvary exalted and Christ magnified, the Gospel is preached."[231]

Spurgeon refused to allow others to dictate the subject of his preaching. He said, "My motto is 'I yield to none.' I preach what I like, when I like, and as I like."[232] Spurgeon (and Paul) not only preached to evangelize and edify but to counsel. Where counsel is given in the pulpit, less time for counseling will be expended in the study. And the counsel given in private will stem from the counseling shared in the pulpit. They are intertwined.

A sidebar: preachers must preach, for that is their primary call. Put them in any other saddle and the ride is not as comfortable or as effective. Spurgeon found this to be the case personally. In the lecture "Sermons in Candles," he said, "I am not adept at lecturing, and when I take to it under constraint, I either signally fail in it, or else the successful production is a sermon in disguise. You cannot drive out nature by command; the old pulpit hand must preach, even though you bid him do somewhat else."[233] Amen and amen.

A father took his son to the church where the father had been saved through loud gospel preaching many years earlier. Inside the church, the boy noticed a rope hanging from the ceiling and asked his father about it. The father shared that it was the rope that pulled the bell in the steeple to call the people to church to hear the Gospel and get saved. The boy looked up at him and said, "Daddy, ring it again!" O preacher, ring the bell of salvation. Ring it again and again and again.[234]

Ringing it will infuse stamina to endure suffering as a good soldier of Christ. "To any brother who says, 'I do not know how I can preach more Gospel than I do, for I preach very often,' I would reply, 'You need not preach oftener, but fill the sermons fuller of the Gospel.'"[235]

Note: despite popular belief that Spurgeon never gave a "come forward" evangelistic invitation, Eric Hayden, in *Searchlight on Spurgeon,* cites evidence to the contrary; he did, though not regularly.[236] Hayden was told stories by his grandfather of the famed preacher often giving public appeals to respond to the sermon in the church. Available floor space in the Tabernacle wasn't conducive to the response of hundreds up front, so people were told to go to the basement lecture halls where counseling would take place with the elders.[237] Lewis Drummond said that Spurgeon at times extended a public appeal to come forward and cites an article in *The Sword and The Trowel* of 1865 to document it.[238] Hayden also told of a time that Spurgeon knelt and prayed with an inquirer in front of the lecture hall.[239] (Eric Hayden attended the Metropolitan Tabernacle and later became its pastor.)

16
The Peril of Souls

"The truest reward of our life work is to bring dead souls to life. I long to see souls brought to Jesus every time I preach. It should break my heart if I did not see it to be so. Men are passing into eternity so rapidly that we must have them saved at once."[240]

~ C. H. Spurgeon

> Principle: The eternal punishment that awaits the unsaved in Hell motivates the preacher not to faint in ministry.

"Therefore seeing we have this ministry [to bring the lost to Christ], as we have received mercy, we faint not" (2 Corinthians 4:1). Paul says in Romans 9:1–3 and 10:1 that his driving force in the ministry was the salvation of the lost. It continually put wind in his sails. He testifies, "I am made all things to all men, that I might by all means save some" (1 Corinthians 9:22). And again he declares, "So I am willing to endure anything if it will bring salvation and eternal glory in Christ Jesus to those God has chosen" (2 Timothy 2:10 NLT). Commenting on this text, Matthew Henry said, "Next to the salvation of our own souls [as it was with Paul], we should be willing to do and suffer anything to promote the salvation of the souls of others."[241]

W. A. Criswell states, "Remarkable elasticity is necessary in the major task of evangelism. Paul concludes a long sentence emphasizing his own mode of life by stressing that he had 'become all things to all,' so that he might be effective in reaching some. The statement implies absolutely no compromise of theological or moral truths, but flexibility in methodology."[242]

Saith Spurgeon, "He [Paul] did not carry about with him one sermon for all places but adapted his speech to his audience. All men are not to be reached in the same way or by the same means."[243] With regard to continuation in the ministry he said, "For necessity is laid upon me; yea, woe is unto me, if I preach not the gospel [if I abandon ship or preach something else]" (1 Corinthians 9:16). "This necessity was a force working from within, not a pressure from without."[244] It's this "necessity" that keeps Paul and Spurgeon and you and me in the ministry. For "if our gospel be hid [if we faint], it is hid to them that are lost" (2 Corinthians 4:3).

Saving the lost by "snatching them from the fire" (Jude 23 CSB) was Spurgeon's incentive for not quitting the ministry. In his autobiography he said, "One of my happiest thoughts is that when I die, it shall be my privilege to enter into rest in the bosom of Christ, and I know that I shall not enjoy my Heaven alone. Thousands have already entered there who have been drawn to Christ under my ministry. Oh! what bliss it will be to fly to Heaven and to have a multitude of converts before and behind."[245] (What a motivation for every minister to persevere in the work!)

In the sermon "Preach the Gospel," he addresses the preacher with words that echoed the passion of his heart: "Oh, minister of the Gospel! stand for one moment and bethink thyself of thy poor fellow creatures! See them like a stream, rushing to eternity...to the pit. Oh, minister, bethink thyself that men are being damned each hour by thousands and that each time thy pulse beats another soul lifts up its eyes in Hell, being in torments. I say, is there not a necessity laid upon thee? Is it not woe unto thee if thou preachest not the Gospel?"[246]

It was compassion for the unsaved that prompted God to send Jesus to earth, and that which enabled Him to endure even the death on the Cross for their rescue. And compassion will be the preacher's incentive to keep preaching when all of Hell wants him to quit (Matthew 9:36). Compassion for the dying lost and hurting saint will keep the preacher ministering through criticism, slander, abandonment, ridicule, suffering and false accusation.

In *Lectures to My Students,* Spurgeon explains why the preacher mustn't quit. He states, "Consider the great evil which will certainly come upon us and upon our hearers if we be negligent in our work. 'They shall perish'—is not that a dreadful sentence? It is to me quite as awful as that which follows it: 'but their blood will I require at the watchman's hand.' How shall we describe the doom of an unfaithful minister? And every unearnest minister is unfaithful. I would infinitely prefer to be consigned to Tophet [a term for Hell] as a murderer of men's bodies than as a destroyer of men's souls; neither do I know of any condition in which a man can perish so fatally, so infinitely, as in that of the man who preaches a Gospel which he does not believe and assumes the office of pastor over a people whose good he does not intensely desire. Let us pray to be found faithful always and ever."[247]

Spurgeon's (and Paul's) vigor in working to the end is attributed to the eternal damnation of the lost. "Let us endure," Spurgeon said, "every cross, and despise all shame, for the joy which Jesus sets before us of winning men for him."[248] "Work for Jesus keeps us strong in faith and intense in love for Him. Soul winning keeps the heart lively and preserves our warm youth in Christ."[249]

A great preacher testified that when his heart became "cold," he would go soul winning, and immediately it would be warmed. It would be nigh impossible for a minister who pursues souls passionately to 'grow weary in well doing' and desert his post.

Not "Can I prove that I ought to go?" but "Can I prove that I ought not to go?" When a man can prove honestly that he ought not to go, then he is clear, but not else.
Charles Spurgeon

Note: Spurgeon's burden for souls (which inflamed his soul not to *faint*) extended beyond London unto all the world. The burden is expressed in a lecture delivered to the "preacher boys" at the Pastor's College: "Hundreds of millions have seen a missionary only once in their lives and know nothing of our King. Shall we let them perish? Can we go to our beds and sleep while China, India, Japan, and other nations are being damned? Are we clear of their blood? Have they no claim upon us? We ought to put it on this footing—not 'Can I prove that I ought to go?' but 'Can I prove that I ought not to go?' When a man can prove honestly that he ought not to go, then he is clear, but not else. What answer do you give, my brethren? I put it to you man by man. I am not raising a question among you which I have not honestly put to myself. I have felt that if some of our leading ministers would go forth it would have a grand effect in stimulating the churches, and I have honestly asked myself whether I ought to go. After balancing the whole thing, I feel bound to keep my place, and I think the judgment of most Christians would be the same; but I hope I would cheerfully go if it were my duty to do so. Brethren, put yourselves through the same process."[250]

Can you prove that you ought to go or not to go? "If you feel a call to India, seek to prove it by working successfully at home first, for India stands in no need of men who would be useless in England."[251] (Spurgeon early on considered foreign missionary service.)

17
Disposition Never to Cower

"We cannot consent to be gagged. There is no reason why we should be. We will go to no place where we cannot take our Master with us. While others take liberty to sin, we shall not renounce our liberty to rebuke and warn them."[252]

~ C. H. Spurgeon

> Principle: Courage and boldness underpin the minister's ability to stand firm.

Don't cower down. Don't cool down. Don't come down. Don't back down. A. W. Tozer said, "The true follower [minister] of Christ will not ask, 'If I embrace this truth, what will it cost me?' Rather he will say, 'This is truth. God help me walk in it, let come what may!'"[253]

Luther states, "A preacher must be both soldier and shepherd. He must nourish, defend, and teach; he must have teeth in his mouth and be able to bite and fight." What a descriptive picture both statements are about Paul, who said, "For I am not ashamed of the gospel" (Romans 1:16). *Retreat* was not in Paul's vocabulary. Despite threats and attacks meant to silence him, he maintained an undaunted courage (Acts 20:23; 2 Corinthians 11:23–27) that was granted by the Holy Spirit (Acts 20:22). He requested the Ephesus saints to pray that he might be infused with boldness (Ephesians 6:19).

E. M. Bounds states, "He desired them to pray that he might have boldness. No quality seems more important to the preacher than that of boldness. It is that positive quality which does not reckon consequences, but with freedom and fullness meets the crisis, faces a present danger, and discharges unawed a present duty. It was one of the marked characteristics of apostolic preachers and apostolic preaching. They were bold men; they were bold preachers. The reference to the manifestation of the principle by them is almost the record of their trials. It is the applause of their faith. There are many chains which enslave the preacher. His very tenderness makes him weak. His attachments to the people tend to bring him into bondage. His personal intercourse, his obligations to his people, his love for them, all tend to hamper his freedom and restrain his pulpit deliverances. What great need to be continually praying for boldness to speak boldly as he ought to speak!"[254]

Saith Spurgeon, "Conceit is to be dreaded, but so is cowardice."[255] Spurgeon told his people, "There is one sin which I believe I have never committed. I think that I have never been afraid of any of you, and I hope, by the grace of God, that I never shall be. If I dare not speak the truth on all points and dare not rebuke sin, what is the good of me to you?"[256]

Saith Spurgeon, "A trembling lip and a coward countenance in a minister show him to be unworthy of the office which he pretends to sustain. We must set our faces like a flint and bear testimony to the truth—to the whole truth, and nothing but the truth, as far as God shall teach it to us."[257] "We are called, not to flirt with error," he remarked, "but to fight with it; therefore, let us be brave and push on the conflict."[258] See Jude 3.

And this Spurgeon personally did. He cowered before no man or ecclesiastical body. His pulpit boldness was no more highly displayed than in the Rivulet controversy in 1856 (combatted doctrinal heresy in a hymnal), the Baptismal Regeneration debate in 1864, and the Down-Grade Controversy in 1887–1891.[259]

Spurgeon, during those times especially, reminds us of Luther, who at the Diet of Worms with his life in the balance, refused to recant what he had written (the 95 theses and writings of his other teachings), saying, "My conscience is captive to the Word of God. Thus, I cannot and will not recant, because acting against one's conscience is neither safe nor sound. Here I stand; I can do no other. God help me"; and of Cyprian, who in route to suffering martyrdom was offered extended time to weigh whether it was better for him to cast a grain of incense into the fire in honor of idols or to die a degraded death on behalf of his God. He responded, "There needs no deliberation in the case."

No deliberation ever was needed by Spurgeon about what to do when threatened with reprisal for standing true to his biblical convictions. In the earliest controversy (Rivulet) Spurgeon wrote, "We shall soon have to handle truth, not with kid gloves, but with gauntlets—the gauntlets of holy courage and integrity. Go on, ye warriors of the cross, for the King is at the head of you."[260] He was a prophet in his own time, for that which he foresaw soon happened.

Of the Down-Grade Controversy he stated, "One thing is clear to us: we cannot be expected to meet in any Union which comprehends those whose teaching is on fundamental points exactly the reverse of that which we hold dear....To us it appears that there are many things upon which to compromise is possible, but there are others in which it would be an act of treason to pretend to fellowship."[261] Later he said, "To pursue union at the expense of truth is treason to the Lord Jesus";[262] and, "A loyal man is not at home in the company of traitors."[263]

Spurgeon's complaint with the Baptist Union was three-fold. That the plenary inspiration of the Scriptures (every part of Scripture—doctrine, history, geography, dates, names—is God-given and without error; inerrancy) was rebuffed and the Bible undermined. That the vicarious death of Christ was not preached, and thus the means of salvation were left unclear. That the doctrine of future punishment had been supplanted with a teaching of universal restoration.[264]

In the monthly *The Sword and the Trowel*, he surmised the conflict: "Our warfare is with men who are giving up the atoning sacrifice, denying the inspiration of Holy Scripture, and casting slurs upon justification by faith. The present struggle is not a debate upon the question of Calvinism or Arminianism, but of the truth of God versus the inventions of men. All who believe the Gospel should unite against that 'modern thought' which is its deadly enemy."[265]

I would rather stand alone in the light of truth than in the crowd filled with error.
Adrian Rogers

Remarks Spurgeon: "Dare to be a Daniel. Our great Captain should be served by brave soldiers. What a reason for bravery is here! God is with those who are with Him. God will never be away when the hour of struggle comes. Do they threaten you? Who are you that you should be afraid of a man that shall die? Will you lose your situation? Your God whom you serve will find bread and water for His servants. Can you not trust Him? Do they pour ridicule upon you? Will this break your bones or your heart? Bear it for Christ's sake, and even rejoice because of it. Fear to fear. Be afraid to be afraid. Your worst enemy is within your own bosom. Get to your knees and cry for help, and then rise up, saying, 'I will trust, and not be afraid.'"[266]

To the pastor that suffers adversity and affliction for opposing the wrong and standing for the right, Spurgeon provides encouragement. "If you do what is right, it looks as if you will be great losers and great sufferers; believe this: God can deliver you. He can prevent your having to suffer what you suppose you may; and if He does not prevent that, He can help you to bear it, and, in a short time, He can turn all your losses into gains, all your sufferings into happiness. He can make the worst thing that can happen to you to be the very best thing that ever did happen to you. If you are serving God, you are serving an Omnipotent Being; and that Omnipotent Being will not leave you in the time of difficulty, but He will come to your rescue. Many of us can say with Paul, 'We trust not in ourselves, but in God which raiseth the dead: who delivered us from so great a death, and doth deliver: in whom we trust that he will yet deliver us.' The Lord has helped us in the past, He is helping us in the present, and we believe that He will help us all the way through. I believe that we have reason to expect interpositions of providence to help us when we are called to suffer for Christ's sake."[267]

William Gurnall said, "A minister without boldness is like a smooth file, a knife without an edge, a sentinel that is afraid to let off his gun. If men will be bold in sin, ministers must be bold to reprove."[268] Socrates remarks, "He is a man of courage who does not run away, but remains at his post and fights against the enemy."[269]

Spurgeon challenges, "Do not turn your back like a coward, but play the man. Follow boldly in your Master's steps, for He has made this rough journey before you."[270] See Proverbs 28:1b. "The fearful and fainthearted," writes Spurgeon, "dishonor their God. Besides, what a bad example it is."[271]

18
Firm Confidence in God

"Man has done much, but there is a limit to his power; and let him not boast of what he can do, for his strength is but derived from the Omnipotent."[272]

~ C. H. Spurgeon

> Principle: The minister's security against faltering is distrust of self and absolute trust in God.

Paul and Spurgeon refused to rely upon the flesh in their ministerial duties and Christian walk. Paul states, "For we...have no confidence in the flesh" (Philippians 3:3). Paul learned not to put confidence in himself—his giftedness, attainments, apostolic office, religious pedigree, knowledge, and past successes. His confidence remained steadfast only in Christ (Ephesians 3:12; Philippians 1:6). Note: if any man might put confidence in the flesh, it was Paul, but even he dared not to do so (Philippians 3:4).

The arm of flesh will fail you;
You dare not trust your own.

~ George Duffield (1858)

Spurgeon urged "preacher boys": "Be not self-sufficient. Think yourselves nothing, for you are nothing; and live by

God's help. The way to grow strong in Christ is to become weak in yourself. God pours no power into man's heart till man's power is all poured out. Live then daily a life of dependence on the grace of God."[273] In the sermon "Hold Fast Your Shield," he addresses how a person might cast away their confidence in Christ (Hebrews 10:35): "You can cast it away by changing it for self-confidence. You can get off from the platform on which you now stand, which is that of simple confidence in your Savior, and you can very readily grow confident in yourselves."[274] And it's that self-reliance that brings disheartenment and defeat in trial.

> Tho' heavy woes come down,
> Tho' Satan seems to reign,
> Tho' God upon me seem to frown,
> I'll trust Him just the same.
>
> ~ A. J. Scarborough (1901)

Spurgeon continues, "The spirit that is to sustain infirmity is not a spirit of doubt and fear and mistrust. There is no power about such a spirit as that; it is like a body without bone or sinew or muscle. Strength lieth in believing. He who can trust can work; he who can trust can suffer. The spirit that can sustain a man in his infirmity is the spirit that can say, 'Though he slay me, yet will I trust in him; come what may, I will not doubt my God, for His word is strong and steadfast.'"[275]

The preacher's "rock of Gibraltar" of endurance and hope in the storm is in displaying unwavering trust in Christ, who will not fail or forsake him (Deuteronomy 31:6). "We are not to cross a trackless desert," said Spurgeon weeks prior to his death; "the Lord has ordained our path in His infallible wisdom and infinite love. 'The steps of a good man are ordered by the Lord; and He delighteth in his way.'"[276]

19

Anchored to the Promises

"There is not a promise—not a word in the Bible—that is not ours. In the depths of tribulation, it will comfort. In the midst of waves of distress, it will cheer; when sorrows surround, it will be our helper."[277]

~ C. H. Spurgeon

> Principle: The promises of God provide a sure footing in the difficulties and trials of ministry.

In seasons of hardship, Paul and Spurgeon anchored their lives and ministries unwaveringly in the promises of God. Paul said, "For no matter how many promises God has made, they are 'Yes' in Christ. And so through him the 'Amen' is spoken by us to the glory of God" (2 Corinthians 1:20 NIV). He claimed God's promise of added grace to bear the suffering and hardship of his "thorn in the flesh" (2 Corinthians 12:9), as well as that which was heaped upon him by others.

In Romans 8, Paul cites promises God gave him that sustained him in struggle and storm: "Nay, in all these things we are more than conquerors through him that loved us. For I am persuaded, that neither death, nor life, nor angels, nor principalities, nor powers, nor things present, nor things to come, Nor height, nor depth, nor any other creature, shall be able to separate us from the love of God, which is in Christ Jesus our Lord" (vv. 37–39), and, "We have sufferings now. But the sufferings we have now are nothing compared to the great glory that will be given to us" (v. 18 ICB).

Spurgeon declared, "A promise from the mouth of God is better than a bond signed and sealed by the wealthiest of men."[278] In the sermon "A Description of Young Men in Christ," Spurgeon asserts, "The promises of God's Word, too—what power they give a man. To get a hold of a 'shall' and 'will' in the time of trouble is a heavenly safeguard. 'My God will hear me.' 'I will not fail thee nor forsake thee.' These are divine holdfasts. Oh, how strong a man is for overcoming the wicked one when he has such a promise to hand! Do not trust yourself in the morning in the street till you have laid a promise under your tongue."[279]

And that's what he did in adversity. He declared, "God has given no pledge which He will not redeem and encouraged no hope which He will not fulfill. I believe all of God's promises, but many of them I have personally tried and proven. I have seen that they are true, for they have been fulfilled to me. I have endured tribulation from many sides. Sharp bodily pain succeeded mental depression, and this was accompanied both by bereavement and affliction in the person of one as dear as life [Susannah]. Never were the promises of Jehovah so precious to me as at this hour. Some of them I never understood until now, for I was not myself mature enough to perceive their meaning. How much more wonderful is the Bible to me now than it was a few months ago! In obeying the Lord, I have not received new promises; but the result to me is much the same, for the old ones have opened up to me with richer stores."[280]

> There is a promise prepared for your present emergencies.
> Charles Spurgeon

Fitting are words of encouragement to the struggling pastor shared by Spurgeon in *Faith's Checkbook:* "He will bear you through. There is a promise prepared for your present emergencies; and if you will believe and plead it at the mercy-seat through Jesus Christ, you shall see the hand of the Lord stretched out to help you. Everything else will fail, but His Word never will. He has been so faithful to me in countless instances that I must encourage you to trust Him too."[281]

He promised to keep me, support and defend me,
When trials o'ertake and temptations assail;
He promised to guide me, and I am persuaded
His promises never, no, never can fail.
~ William C. Poole (1912)

Henry Ward Beecher said, "There are promises in *God's Word* that no man has ever tried to find. There are treasures of gold and silver in it that no man has taken the pains to dig for. There are medicines in it, for the want of a knowledge of which hundreds have died. There is many a promise of God that is strong enough to carry men across the abyss of this life, but they do not dare to try it. In an emergency, the promises of God are to many men what weapons of defense are to a man who does not know how to use them when he finds that he must fight for his life."[282]

Spurgeon tells how he appropriated the promises: "In my time of trouble I like to find a promise which exactly fits my need, and then to put my finger on it and say, 'Lord, this is Thy word; I beseech Thee to prove that it is so by carrying it out in my case. I believe that this is Your own writing, and I pray Thee make it good to my faith.' I believe in plenary inspiration, and I humbly look to the Lord for a plenary fulfillment of every sentence that He has put on record."[283]

Adrian Rogers says, "Wait before God until you get a promise, and let that promise come out of the Word of God. We are not meant to take confidence in ourselves, but we can always take confidence in God and His promises."[284]

Standing on the promises that cannot fail,
When the howling storms of doubt and fear assail,
By the living Word of God I shall prevail,
Standing on the promises of God.
~ Russell Kelso Carter (1886)

In the sermon "Not Bound Yet," Spurgeon said, "If there is a promise of deliverance to you and you cannot see the way in which you are to be delivered, you may not, therefore, doubt the promise, for that would dishonor the Lord who spoke it."[285]

Remember, as Spurgeon asserts, "The living word is on the way from the living God, and though it may seem to linger, it is not in reality doing so. God's train is not behind time. It is only a matter of patience, and we shall soon see for ourselves the faithfulness of the Lord. No promise of His shall fail: 'it will not lie.' No promise of His will be lost in silence: 'it shall speak' (Habakkuk 2:3)."[286]

"As you read them over one after the other," saith Spurgeon, "you say to yourselves, *This is my checkbook. I can take out the promises as I want them, sign them by faith, present them at the great Bank of Grace, and come away enriched with present help in time of need.* That is the way to use God's promises."[287]

20

Future Glory

"A hope of Heaven is a mighty strengthener for bearing the ills of life and the persecutions of the adversary."[288]

~ C. H. Spurgeon

Principle: The hope of Heaven incites perseverance to the end.

To the Corinthian church, Paul gives reason for his tenacity in ministry: "So we do not give up. Our physical body is becoming older and weaker, but our spirit inside us is made new every day. We have small troubles for a while now, but they are helping us gain an eternal glory that is much greater than the troubles. We set our eyes not on what we see but on what we cannot see. What we see will last only a short time, but what we cannot see will last forever" (2 Corinthians 4:16–18 NCV). And he said, "We are filled with hope, as we wait for the glorious return of our great God and Savior Jesus Christ" (Titus 2:13 CEV).

Warren Wiersbe says, "Because he had this kind of confidence, Paul was not afraid of suffering and trials, or even of dangers. He walked by faith and not by sight. He looked at the eternal unseen, not the temporal seen (2 Corinthians 4:18). Heaven was not simply a destination for Paul; it was a motivation."[289] Another writer comments, "It filled him with the fortitude to endure, with boldness and strength to do."[290]

Though the outward man is 'perishing' or wasting away (2 Corinthians 4:16) and is constantly being battered by evil men, the assuring confidence of eternal life in Heaven with God (based upon the eternal verities of God and His Holy Word, not "blind faith") instills boldness, and motivation to finish the race strong (Romans 8:23–25). See 1 Thessalonians 1:3; Colossians 1:5. Saith Paul, "What we are suffering now is nothing compared with our future glory. Everything God created looks forward to the future. That will be the time when his children appear in their full and final glory" (Romans 8:18–19 NIRV). See Colossians 1:23.

In *Morning and Evening,* Spurgeon asserts, "Zeal is also stimulated by the thought of the eternal future. It looks with tearful eyes down to the flames of Hell, and it cannot slumber; it looks up with anxious gaze to the glories of Heaven, and it cannot but bestir itself. It feels that time is short compared with the work to be done, and therefore it devotes all that it has to the cause of its Lord."[291]

The first incentive for perseverance (to keep man out of Hell) is treated in another chapter. Here we address the latter, Heaven. Saith Spurgeon: "Whether it be for hope, for joy, for consolation, or for the inspiring of our love, the future must, after all, be the grand object of the eye of faith. Looking into the future, we see sin cast out, the body of sin and death destroyed, the soul made perfect and fit to be a partaker of the inheritance of the saints in light. Looking further yet, the believer's enlightened eye can see death's river passed, the gloomy stream forded, and the hills of light attained on which standeth the celestial city; he seeth himself enter within the pearly gates, hailed as more than conqueror, crowned by the hand of Christ, embraced in the arms of Jesus, glorified with Him, and made to sit together with Him on His throne, even as He has overcome and has sat down with the Father on His throne. The thought of this future may well relieve the darkness of the past and the gloom of the present."[292]

In the sermon "The Hope Laid Up in Heaven," Spurgeon said, "'It will soon be over,' says a man who looks for Heaven, and therefore he is not over-weighted with grief. 'It is an ill lodging,' said the traveler, 'but I shall be away in the morning.' Well may we be strengthened with all might by the hope of Heaven; it is but reason that the exceeding weight of glory should cast into the shade this light affliction, which is but for a moment."[293]

And in "The Hope of Future Bliss," he says of the hope of Heaven, "Why, this is the highest motive that can actuate a man. I suppose this was what made Luther so bold, when he stood before his great audience of kings and lords, and said, 'I stand by the truth that I have written, and will so stand by it till I die; so help me God!' For this the missionary ventures the stormy sea; for this he treads the barbarous shore; for this he goes into inhospitable climes and risks his life, because he knows there is a payment to come by-and-by."[294]

Further, in the sermon "The Anchor," he states, "Brethren, do you know anything about your hope holding you? It will hold you if it is a good hope; you will not be able to get away from it, but under temptation and depression of spirit, and under trial and affliction, you will not only hold your hope, that is your duty, but your hope will hold you, that is your privilege."[295] Saith Spurgeon, "Is there nothing to sing about today? Then borrow a song from tomorrow; sing of what is yet to be. Is this world dreary? Then think of the next."[296]

Is there nothing to sing about today? Then borrow a song from tomorrow; sing of what is yet to be. Is this world dreary? Then think of the next.

Charles Spurgeon

Timothy Keller said, "We need a living hope to get through life and endure suffering. A living hope enables us to have both sorrow and joy."[297] Let the minister cultivate his hope of Heaven, and it will enable endurance through the valley of Baca (Psalm 84:6). John Piper cautions, "One of the great enemies of hope is forgetting God's promises."[298]

And when I'm to die, "Receive me," I'll cry,
For Jesus hath loved me; I cannot say why.
But this I do find: we two are so joined,
He'll not live in Glory and leave me behind.[299]

~ John Gambold (1742)

Two ministers in London crossed paths en route to their perspective churches to preach one Sunday. The one had a rustic chapel wherein to preach, the other a far better place. He of the far bigger church asked him of the smaller what he expected for his preaching. "Well," he said, "I expect to have a crown."

"Ah!" said the other preacher, "I have not been in the habit of preaching for less than a guinea, anyhow."

"Oh!" said the other, "I am obliged to be content with a crown, and what is more, I do not have my crown now, but I have to wait for that in the future."[300] The minister had no idea that he meant the "crown of life that fadeth not away!" But we do, and it is an incentive to press on despite the desire to quit in times of grave trial and suffering.

Saith Spurgeon, "On the glory yet to be revealed, on the glories of the Second Advent, especially, often dwell; and let your hearts take fire as you think of them, and let your spirit grow strong with an intense delight, because HE is coming. HE is coming quickly; and who knows when He may appear? Live upon the promise of His coming, and rejoice therein."[301]

21
Avoidance of Presumption

"He who thinks he stands is not likely to keep his footing if he fears no fall, nor guards against it."[302]

~ Matthew Henry

Principle: Overestimation of one's strength and stamina prompts stumbling.

Adversity tests the mettle of perceived (assumed) strength and sometimes we are found lacking. Spurgeon said, "I gravely question whether some of us will find our vessels, when far out at sea, to be quite so seaworthy as we think them. Prove your own selves, and may the Lord prepare you for the crucible and the furnace which assuredly await you."[303]

The ship must be built for the storm, not just the calm. See 2 Corinthians 6:2–10. We learn from Peter that perceived strength may be hollow. Boasting of strength, he professed that he would never deny the Lord, yet upon facing the test, he failed it three times (Matthew 26:34–35). See Proverbs 24:10.

David's boast was likewise hollow when he exclaimed, "I shall never be moved" (Psalm 30:6). Matthew Henry comments, "His mountain was shaken and he with it; it proved, when he grew secure, that he was least safe."[304] Saith

Spurgeon, "He [David] stood by grace, and yet forgot himself, and so met with a fall. Reader, is there not much of the same proud stuff in all our hearts? Let us beware lest the fumes of intoxicating success get into our brains and make fools of us also."[305]

Past victories in adversity and temptation bring no guarantees into tomorrow's battles. To the contrary, presumption is fatal. He who boasts of resiliency in trials and hardships and invulnerability to temptation is self-deluded and will stumble. Take heed: "Pride goeth before...a fall." (A self-sufficient attitude precedes stumbling.)

Spurgeon exhorts, "I warn you against that evil thing, a false confidence and presumption which creepeth over a Christian like the cold death-sleep on the mountain-top, from which, if he is not awakened, death will be the inevitable consequence." [306] Further, he says, "Take heed to yourself lest in aught you say 'This is Babylon that I have builded'; for remember, both trowel and mortar must come from Him. The life, the voice, the talent, the imagination, the eloquence—all are the gift of God; and he who has the greatest gifts must feel that unto God belongs the shield of the mighty, for He has given might to His people and strength unto His servants."[307]

> If sin could drag an angel from the skies, it may well pluck a minister from the pulpit.
>
> Charles Spurgeon

The preacher must take heed with regard to sin. Don't underestimate sin's power to entice, deceive, and destroy. Spurgeon warns, "If sin could drag an angel from the skies, it may well pluck a minister from the pulpit, a deacon from the Communion Table, a Church member out of the midst of his brethren."[308] "Wherefore," asserts Paul to all that minister, "let him that thinketh he standeth take heed lest he fall" (1 Corinthians 10:12).

And Spurgeon says, "Thy wisest way is to believe thyself neither to be wise nor strong, and therefore to lie humbly at His feet who can make thee both wise and strong, and to look away from thyself up to Him who will keep the feet of His saints. It ought to cool the hot blood of self-conceit in any man to remind him that, although he thinketh that he standeth, it is simply because he has not been tempted as others have been who have fallen; or, if he has been tempted in a way which overthrew them, while he has stood fast, yet, if the temptations were still further increased and he were left to himself, he would find that at the last the fierce wind from the pit would sweep him off his feet even as it has swept off other men who thought that they could never be moved."[309]

He that *thinks* he stands ought to take heed for "such thinking, as it leads to trust in oneself, is the beginning of a perilous security."[310] Saith Albert Barnes, "Those are most safe who feel that they are weak and feeble, and who feel their need of divine aid and strength. They will then rely on the true source of strength, and they will be secure."[311]

Matthew Henry comments, "The harms sustained by others should be cautious to us. He that thinks he stands should not be confident and secure, but upon his guard. Others have fallen, and so may we. And then we are most likely to fall when we are most confident of our own strength, and thereupon most apt to be secure and off our guard. Distrust of himself, putting him at once upon vigilance and dependence on God, is the Christian's best security."[312]

Spurgeon gives warning, "Those who think themselves secure are men more exposed to danger than any others. Count no place, however secret, a sanctuary from sin! Satan can climb housetops and enter closets, and even if we could shut him out, that foul fiend, our own corruptions are enough to work our ruin unless grace prevent."[313] Just ask King David if that is not so! Saith Spurgeon, "How many that flamed like comets in the sky of the religious world have been quenched in darkness!"[314]

Spurgeon's means of thwarting presumptuous self-confidence is revealed in the counsel he gave to others about defeating it. "Take heed that thou gloriest not in thy graces, but let all thy glorying and confidence be in Christ and His strength, for only so canst thou be kept from falling. Be much more in prayer. Spend longer time in holy adoration. Read the Scriptures more earnestly and constantly. Watch your lives more carefully. Live nearer to God. Take the best examples for your pattern. Let your conversation be redolent of Heaven. Let your hearts be perfumed with affection for men's souls. So live that men may take knowledge of you that you have been with Jesus. On, Christian, with care and caution! On with holy fear and trembling! On with faith and confidence in Jesus alone, and let your constant petition be, 'Uphold me according to Thy word.' He is able, and He alone 'to keep you from falling, and to present you faultless before the presence of his glory with exceeding joy.'"[315]

22
No Labor Is in Vain

"The due season for harvest is not the day after the seed-sowing, but we must wait awhile and not be weary. The harvest will come as the Lord appoints."[316]

~ C. H. Spurgeon

Principle: No work for Christ is wasted or futile, even if it appears barren.

Like Paul, Spurgeon's incentive in ministry was a firm belief that no labor for Christ was in vain, despite the absence of visible results. To the congregation at Metropolitan Tabernacle he said, "I do not come into this pulpit myself with any fear that I shall preach in vain. It does not occur to me that such a thing can happen. I thought so once, when I thought more of myself than now; but now I am assured that if I speak out God's message in the best way I can, and with much prayer leave it all with God, he will take care of it."[317]

The effect of the preacher's sowing (preaching, witnessing, teaching) is not always immediate or visible. But he may be confident that the seed (Word of God) sown will 'not return unto God void but it shall accomplish that which He pleases, and it shall prosper in the thing whereto He sent it' (Isaiah 55:11). The power of God's Word assures that no man is left untouched or unchanged when hearing it (Hebrews 4:12).

Solomon gives this truth emphasis in saying, "Cast thy bread upon the waters: for thou shalt find it after many days" (Ecclesiastes 11:1). Sowing, he says, always results in reaping. Our part in labor, saith Solomon, is to use the right seed ("thy bread," the seed of the Gospel [Matthew 13:37]), sow vigilantly ("cast," throw, plant or send out the seed) in the place divinely assigned ("upon the waters," wherever duty beckons, whether favorable or not) and then patiently trust God for a promised harvest ("shall find it [it's not lost!] after many days").

Spurgeon said, "The reaping time will come. The harvest will come in due season. When it comes, it will abundantly repay us." Paul states, "We shall reap, if we faint not" (Galatians 6:9), and it is 'God that gives the increase' (1 Corinthians 3:6). No believer is able to manufac-ture fruit ("give the increase") or cause a single seed to spring up sooner than when God ordains.

And the psalmist declared that they that scatter precious (valuable) seed "shall doubtless come again with rejoicing, bringing his sheaves with him" (Psalm 126:6). Upon the text

Spurgeon comments, "*Doubtless* you will gather sheaves from your sowing. Because the Lord has written *doubtless*, take heed that you do not doubt. No reason for doubt can remain after the Lord has spoken."[318]

H. Edwards says, "The published Word, being assimilated into the human mind, fashions thought, molds character, regenerates life; and therefore it does not return void to its Author. And even though it should be humanly rejected, it still would not return void; individual hearing creates individual responsibility, and hence leaves no one in the same place."[319]

A missionary shared a tract with a young man, urging him to be saved. When the missionary left, the youth thrust the tract into the fire. As the pages of the tract curled up in the fire, he saw the words "Heaven and earth shall pass away, but My words shall not pass away." The words ignited a fire in his soul, causing him not to rest until he got saved. Though unseen by the missionary, the Word of God accomplished its purpose.

In the sermon "Christ's Loneliness and Ours," Spurgeon said, "Never mind *where* you work—care more about *how* you work. Never mind who sees or does not see you, as long as God approves your efforts. If He smiles, be content. We cannot be always sure when we are most useful."[320]

A minister's travel to a preaching post was with great difficulty. Deep snow covered the ground and hindered all but one man from attending the service. The preacher, however, delivered his sermon as ardently to that man as if there had been a thousand in the house. Years afterward the minister returned to the town and met the founder of a church in the village from which many other churches had been established. The man said to the preacher, "I have good reason to remember you, sir, for I was once your only hearer. And what has been done here has been brought about instrumentally through my conversion under that sermon."[321]

Saith Spurgeon: "We cannot estimate our success. One child in the Sunday school, converted, may turn out to be worth five hundred others, because he may be the means of bringing ten thousand to Christ. It is not the acreage you sow; it is the multiplication which God gives to the seed which will make up the harvest. You have less to do with being successful than with being faithful. Your main comfort is that in your labor you are not alone, for God, the eternal One who guides the marches of the stars, is with you."[322]

And Melvill wrote, "The minister who has been oppressed up to his dying hour by the melancholy conviction that his warnings, his entreaties, his expostulations have been lost on his congregation may be hailed by many as the instrument of their conversion."[323] Paul exhorts all believers, "Therefore, my beloved brothers, be steadfast, immovable, always abounding in the work of the Lord, knowing that in the Lord your labor is not in vain" (1 Corinthians 15:58 ESV).

If you have labored for Christ with the absence of visible success, do not infer that your work was futile or unproductive. Your part is to sow; it's the Lord's to reap. "And when at the last those who have gladly spent and been spent in the service of God, and whose toils and sacrifices have never been sweetened by the knowledge that they were effectual in accomplishing the ends for which they were endured—when these men shall receive their portion from their Judge, there will be given the most effectual demonstration that 'God is not unrighteous to forget their work of labor and love.' To every man will be allotted a recompense, to every sacrifice a compensation."[324] The Bible says, "For God is not unjust; he will not forget your work and the love you demonstrated for his name by serving the saints—and by continuing to serve them" (Hebrews 6:10 CSB).

Use the right measuring stick to evaluate success in laboring for the Master—not man's perception, but God's promise. Bread cast upon the waters will eventually, now or later, bear fruit. So keep casting your bread upon the waters, despite the nonvisible result. Spurgeon said, "Be it ours to sow, not only on the honest and good soil, but on the rock and on the highway, and at the last great day to reap a glad harvest. May the bread which we cast upon the waters in odd times and strange occasions be found again after many days."[325]

Keep preaching. Keep teaching. Keep witnessing. Keep singing. Keep writing. Keep mentoring. In time ("due season") that which is sown will bear profitability for others, the kingdom, and yourself. "The reaping time will come, therefore thrust in the plow."[326] Hold fast to the Sower's promise. "Those who sow with tears will reap with songs of joy. Those who go out weeping, carrying seed to sow, will return with songs of joy, carrying sheaves with them" (Psalm 126:5–6 NIV).

Spurgeon comments: "We must sow. We may have to sow in the wet weather of sorrow, but we shall reap, and reap in the bright summer season of joy. Let us keep to the work of this present sowing time and find strength in the promise which is here so positively given us. Here is one of the Lord's *shall*s and *will*s; it is freely given both to workers, waiters, and weepers, and they may rest assured that it will not fail: 'in due season they shall reap.'"[327]

He that patiently trusts God for the increase to the seed which is sown "in due season" thwarts disheartenment and fainting over what could be misconstrued as ministerial failure and defeat.

23

Stir Up the Gift

"Fan into flame the gift that is in you."[328]

~ C. H. Spurgeon

> Principle.
> The gift of preaching will degrade by its disuse, misuse or abuse.

Paul urged the young preacher Timothy (and every preacher) to "stir up [keep the fire alive[329]] the gift of God" [preaching[330]] in him—to keep stoking the spiritual fire lest it be quenched or extinguished and decay (2 Timothy 1:6). John Wesley trans-lates the exhortation to say, "I remind thee of stirring up (literally, blowing up the coals into a flame) the gift of God (all the spiritual gifts) which the grace of God has given thee."[331]

The gift was to be stirred up not only by its use, but through the study of and meditation upon the Word, and prayer, so that he might be enabled, with renewed vigor, to perform his duty as a good soldier of Jesus Christ. Paul undoubtedly 'stirred up the gift' in himself continuously, for he testified, "I keep control of my body, and bring it into subjection, lest that by any means, when I have preached to others, I myself should be a castaway" (1 Corinthians 9:27). See Philippians 2:15.

Spurgeon worked hard at his walk with God as well (Philippians 2:12). To the question as to why the pastor needs to stir up his gift, he says in the sermon "Our Gifts, and How to Use Them," "We must stir up our gift because it needs stirring. The gifts and graces of Christian men are like a coal fire which frequently requires stirring as well as feeding with fuel. We should stir up the gift that is in us, because all we shall do when we have stirred ourselves to the utmost, and when the Spirit of God has strengthened us to the highest degree, will still fall far short of what our dear Lord and Master deserves at our hands."[332]

In a lecture to the students at the Pastor's College, he instructed, "Feed the flame, my brother; feed it frequently. Feed it with holy thought and contemplation, especially with thought about your work, your motives in pursuing it, the design of it, the helps that are waiting for you, and the grand results of it if the Lord be with you."[333]

How else might the preacher stir up his gift? Saith Spurgeon, "It stirs one up to preach with all his might, when he has laid before God in prayer his weakness, and the ability which God has given him too, and asked that the weakness may be consecrated to God's glory and the ability accepted to the Lord's praise. Pray over yourself, as it were: put your whole self upon the altar, and then let the drink-offering be the pouring out of your tears before God in prayer that he would be pleased to accept you, to qualify you, to anoint you, to direct you, and bless you in all that you do. This would be the most excellent manner of stirring up the gift that is in you."[334]

"Pray over your gifts," he exhorts; "that is a blessed way of stirring them up—to go before God and spread out your responsibilities before Him. In my own case I have often to cry, 'Lord, Thou hast given me this congregation, and, oh, it is hard to be clear of the blood of them all, and to speak with affection and prudence and courage to all, so as not to leave one unwarned, unhelped, untaught. Help me, my Lord, that I may leave no one without his portion of meat in due season. Who is sufficient for these things? Only Thy grace is sufficient for me."[335]

Additionally, stir up the gift of preaching through the study of the Word. The psalmist said, 'When I mused the fire burned' (Psalm 39:3). "The ministry demands brain labor," saith Spurgeon. "The preacher must throw his thought into his teaching, and read and study to keep his mind in good trim."[336]

Is sermon preparation always an easy task? Spurgeon admitted, "I scarcely ever prepare for my pulpit with pleasure. Study for the pulpit is to me the most irksome work in the world."[337] But he disciplined himself to do it and excelled mightily at it.

As he said, "An idler has no right in the pulpit. He is an instrument of Satan in damning the souls of men."[338] "A man who goes up and down from Monday morning until Saturday night and indolently dreams that he is to have his text sent down by an angelic messenger in that last hour or two of the week tempts God and deserves to stand speechless on the Sabbath,"[339] he charged.

24
Mindset Not to Quit

"The only course open to us is to plow right on to the end of the furrow, and never think of leaving the field till the Master shall call us home."[340]

~ C. H. Spurgeon

> Principle:
> Determination to fight a good fight and finish the course divinely assigned drives the preacher onward through whatever obstacles and troubles are encountered.

"Endure [persevere] unto the end" (Matthew 24:13). Endurance "is that quality of character which does not allow one to surrender to circumstances or succumb under trial."[341] Kenneth Wuest says it is "to remain under trials and testings in a way that honors God."[342] It is to not faint in battle but fight until it's over.

Paul epitomizes endurance. He refused to quit. Determinedly he chose to preach the Word "in season, out of season" (2 Timothy 4:2) until the end. In his last letter he said, "I have fought a good fight, I have finished my course, I have kept the faith" (2 Timothy 4:7).

But neither did Spurgeon quit when things got difficult. He exhorts the minister, "In nothing let us be turned aside from the path which the divine call has urged us to pursue. Come fair or come foul, the pulpit is our watchtower, and the ministry our warfare; be it ours, when we cannot see the face of our God, to trust under THE SHADOW OF HIS WINGS."[343]

Plow through barrenness, suffering, and heartbreak. Preach although it may mean saying with Spurgeon, "I heard my own chains clank while I tried to preach to my fellow prisoners in the dark."[344]

Determine to say with Paul (and Spurgeon) at the close of the day, "I was not disobedient unto the heavenly vision" (Acts 26:19). "Never give in; never give in; never, never, never, never....Never yield to force; never yield to the apparently overwhelming might of the enemy," Winston Churchill exclaimed. Remain at your post until it's done, despite contrary winds (2 Timothy 4:7).

I mean to go right on until the crown is won;
I mean to fight the fight of faith till life on earth is done.
I'll nevermore turn back; defeat I shall not know,
For God will give me victory if onward I shall go.

I'm going on; I'm going on;
Unto the final triumph, I'm going on.
I'm going on; I'm going on;
Unto the final triumph, I'm going on.

Should opposition come, should foes obstruct my way,
Should persecution's fires be lit, as in the ancient day—
With Jesus by my side, His peace within my soul,
No matter if the battle's hot, I mean to win the goal.
~ Charles W. Naylor (1918)

In the sermon "Holding Fast the Faith," Spurgeon gives encouragement to him that plows in barren soil. "O dear children of God, if you are placed in positions of peculiar trial and difficulty, and if your hindrances are so many that you cannot accomplish one-tenth as much as you desire, then hear how Jesus puts it: 'I know where thou dwellest, even where Satan's seat is.' If you are faithful to your Lord and firm in his truth, He will commend you and say, 'Yet thou holdest fast my name, and hast not denied my faith.' I wonder whether this word of comfort is meant for somebody here, or for some friend who will read the sermon. I feel that it must be so. Many of our Lord's beloved ones are, in God's sight, now doing much more, under distressing circumstances, than they used to do in happier days."[345] Keep toiling on. Don't faint. Don't give up. Keep doing what you can despite what you could were the soil more fertile and receptive.

Spurgeon, in a sermon in 1872, asserted, "Happy are they who are preserved from fainting. May this be said of us through a long course of years: 'They labored and fainted not.' When our hair is white with the snows of many winters, may it be said truly by the dear lips of Him who intercedes for us in Heaven, 'Thou hast labored and hast not fainted.' When we lie in our last narrow bed, may this be the encomium [tribute] which our spirit shall hear before the throne of God, 'Thou hast labored and hast not fainted.' May this be such a sentence as an honest affection may dare to write upon our tombs."[346]

"Ready, aye, ready! Ready for storms and ready for calms, ready for whatever Thou dost command, ready for whatever Thou dost ordain!"[347]

The word *quit* wasn't in Spurgeon's vocabulary. Preaching to ministers, he exclaimed, "*Stop preaching! Stop preaching*! Let the sun stop shining, and we will preach in darkness. Let the waves stop their ebb and flow, and still our voice shall preach the Gospel; let the world stop its revolutions, let the planets stay their motion, we will still preach the Gospel. Until the fiery center of this earth shall burst through the thick ribs of her brazen mountains, we shall still preach the Gospel. Till the universal conflagration shall dissolve the earth and matter shall be swept away, these lips, or the lips of some others called of God, shall still thunder forth the voice of Jehovah. We cannot help it. 'Necessity is laid upon us, yea woe is unto us if we preach not the gospel.'"[348] Amen and amen.

"Beloved brethren, we are bound to go forward, cost us what it may, for we dare not go back; we have no armor for our backs. We believe ourselves to be called to this ministry, and we cannot be false to the call."[349]

Beloved brethren, we are bound to go forward, cost us what it may, for we dare not go back; we have no armor for our backs. We believe ourselves to be called to this ministry, and we cannot be false to the call.

Charles Spurgeon

Our times are in Thy hand,
Whatever they may be,
Pleasing or painful, dark or bright,
As best may seem to Thee.

Our times are in Thy hand;
We'll always trust in Thee,
Till we have left this weary land
And all Thy glory see.

~ W. F. Lloyd (1791–1853)

Saith Spurgeon, "Often when we fear we are defeated, we ought to say, 'I will do all the more. Instead of dropping from this work, now will I make a general levy and a sacred conscription upon all the powers of my soul, and I will gather up all the strength I ever had in reserve and make from this moment a tremendous lifelong effort to overcome the powers of darkness and win for Christ fresh trophies of victory.'"[350]

"Hold that fast which thou hast" (Revelation 3:11). Alexander Maclaren says, "The slack hand will very soon be an empty hand. Anybody walking through the midst of a crowd of thieves with a bag of gold in charge would not hold it dangling from a fingertip, but he would put all five around it and wrap the strings about his wrist. The first shape which we may give to this exhortation is hold fast by what God has given in His Gospel; hold fast His Son, His truth, His grace."[351]

And I add, hold fast to thy sacred call and ministry until the beckoning call is heard, "Come; for all things are now ready" (Luke 14:17); "enter thou into the joy of thy Lord" (Matthew 25:23). A timely word comes again from the pen of Spurgeon: "If for a while the evangelicals are doomed to go down, let them die fighting, and in the full assurance that their Gospel will have a resurrection when the inventions of 'modern thought' shall be burned up with fire unquenchable."[352]

"For my name's sake [thou] hast labored, and hast not fainted" (Revelation 2:3). Saith Spurgeon, "Take *Christ,* and believe that He will help thee to go about thy business, to bear thy trouble, to meet thine adversary, to serve without weariness, and to run without fainting."[353] "We must compel ourselves to duty," he says, "when it goes against the grain."[354]

Faint not, *O man of God!* tho' the road
Leading to thy blest abode
Darksome be, and dangerous too—
Christ, thy Guide, will bring thee thro'.

Faint not, *thou man of God!* tho' the world
Hath its hostile flag unfurled.
Hold the cross of Jesus fast;
Thou shalt overcome at last.[355]

~ J. H. Evans (1849)

25

A Literary Interview with Charles Spurgeon

"Lord, we do not tell Thee how to work or what to do; only work like Thyself."[356]

~ C. H. Spurgeon

A literary interview with Charles H. Spurgeon based upon his lectures to students at the Pastor's College, sermons, books, and a monthly magazine, answers pivotal questions about church ministry, preaching, biblical standards, and belief.

Adversity

In a sentence or two, what can you tell us from your experience about suffering?

"Glory be to God for the furnace, the hammer, and the file."[357] "The good I have received from my sorrows and pains and griefs is altogether incalculable. Affliction is the best bit of furniture in my house. It is the best book in a minister's library."[358]

Alcohol

What's your position on strong drink?

"The elixir of life! Ugh! Death and damnation!—that's what that is."[359] "It is the Devil's backdoor to Hell and everything that is hellish, for he that once gives away his brains to drink is ready to be caught by Satan for anything."[360] "Some who are called ministers of Christ have in these days even defended amusements which moralists have felt bound to abandon."[361] "He who does not cry out against the wolf cannot surely be at enmity with the lion."[362] "The best way to make a man sober is to bring him to the foot of the Cross."[363]

What is your opinion of a minister who partakes in alcoholic beverages?

"From a slovenly, smoking, snuff-taking, beer-drinking parson may the church be delivered."[364]

Anonymous Letters

What about anonymous letters?

"I bear witness against all anonymous letters. Never write a letter to which you are ashamed to put your name; as a rule, only mean persons are guilty of such an action, though I hope my present correspondent is an exception to the rule."[365]

Assigned Texts, sermons

If requested to preach upon a certain text, how should the pastor respond?

"[Should] you preach from texts which persons select for you and request you to preach upon? My answer would be, as a rule, never; and if there must be exceptions, let them be few. Receive the request courteously, but if the Lord whom you serve does not cast His light upon the text, do not preach from it, let who may persuade you."[366]

Attire, preacher

How ought the preacher to dress?

"The preacher should endeavor, according to his means, to dress himself respectably; and, as to neatness, he should be without spot, for kings should not have dirty footmen to wait at their table, and they who teach godliness should practice cleanliness. A worn coat is no discredit, but the poorest may be neat. You cannot judge a horse by its harness, but a modest, gentlemanly appearance, in which the dress is just such as nobody could make a remark upon, seems to me to be the right sort of thing."[367]

Baptism

What is baptism and what is its proper method?

"Baptism, the immersion of the believer in water, is the token of his death, burial, and resurrection with Christ. It sets forth the fellowship which he has with his Lord, as the apostle tells us: 'Buried with him in baptism, wherein also ye are risen with him'—not that the plunge into the water confers any grace upon the person who is baptized, but it is the type, the emblem, the instructive symbol of the new birth, which new birth consists in passing, by death and resurrection, into newness of life."[368] "Everyone who is baptized according to the true form laid down in Scripture must be a Trinitarian; otherwise, his baptism is a farce and a lie, and he himself is found a deceiver and a hypocrite before God."[369]

"It is alleged by us, then, that in the ordinance of baptism the candidate should be wholly immersed in water. We appeal to the Scriptures, and appealing to the Scriptures, we find that baptism is, as our text [Colossians 2:12] informs us, a burial and resurrection with Christ, that it is a sign and symbol of the believer's participation in Christ's burial and resurrection, and this I think as plainly as possible shows us what the mode was in ancient times....When we consider that Philip and the eunuch 'went down both of them into the water,' that our Savior 'went up straightway out of the water' after John had baptized him, that John 'was baptizing near Salim because there was much water there,' I think it is very evident that something more than aspersion, or pouring of water, must be implied."[370]

Spurgeon gives a crystal clear reason for his baptism by immersion in his autobiography, Volume 1.[371]

How frequently ought one to be baptized?

"You all know that we are only born once. A thing can only have one true beginning. Hence, baptism is never to be repeated. Once done, it is done forever."[372]

Bible, infallibility

Do you believe the Bible to be totally inerrant?

"The coin of inspiration comes from the mint of infallibility."[373] "You must accept the revelation as infallible, or you cannot unquestioningly believe in the God therein revealed. If you once give up inspiration, the foundations are removed, and all building is laborious trifling. How are the promises the support of faith if they are themselves questionable?[374]

Burials, funeral home directors

What counsel do you give to funeral home directors?

"I hardly think it can be necessary to say that the expending of money on mere show at funerals is absurd, unthrifty, and even cruel. I hope the common sense of the people will soon destroy customs which oppress the widow and fatherless by demanding of them an expenditure which they cannot afford. To bedeck a corpse with vain trappings is a grim unsuitability. Something has been done in the right direction."[375]

Chastening

Is chastening beneficial to the man of God?

"I bear my willing witness that I owe more to the fire and the hammer and the file than to anything else in my Lord's workshop. I sometimes question whether I have ever learned anything except through the rod. When my schoolroom is darkened, I see most."[376]

Children, evangelization

What is the key to the evangelization of children?

"Some...have hindered the children because they have forgotten the child's value. The soul's price does not depend upon its years. Let us recognize the true value of children, and then we won't keep them back, but we shall be eager to lead them to Jesus at once."[377]

Church, the institution

To what purpose does the church exist?

"Churches are not made that men of ready speech may stand up on Sundays and talk, and so win daily bread from their admirers. Nay, there is another end and aim from this. These places of worship are not built that you may sit here comfortably and hear something that shall make you pass away your Sundays with pleasure. A church in London which does not exist to do good in the slums and dens and kennels of the city is a church that has no reason to justify its longer existing. A church that does not exist to reclaim heathenism, to fight with evil, to destroy error, to put down falsehood, a church that does not exist to take the side of the poor, to denounce injustice and to hold up righteousness is a church that has no right to be. Not for yourself, O church, do you exist, any more than Christ existed for Himself. His glory was that

He laid aside His glory, and the glory of the church is when she lays aside her respectability and her dignity and counts it to be her glory to gather together the outcasts, and her highest honor to seek amid the foulest mire the priceless jewels for which Jesus shed His blood. To rescue souls from Hell and lead them to God, to hope, to Heaven, this is her heavenly occupation. Oh, that the church would always feel this! Let her have her bishops and her preachers, and let them be supported, and let everything be done for Christ's sake decently and in order, but let the end be looked to, namely, the conversion of the wandering, the teaching of the ignorant, the help of the poor, the maintenance of the right, the putting down of the wrong, and the upholding at all hazards of the crown and kingdom of our Lord Jesus Christ."[378]

Does the church possess autonomy from the government?

"Let us not be slow with unshaken courage to declare yet again that kings and princes and parliaments have no lawful jurisdiction over the church of Jesus Christ, that it beseems not the best of monarchs to claim those royal prerogatives which God has given to his only begotten Son."[379] "No king, no queen that ever lived, or can live, has any authority whatever over the church of Christ. The church has none to govern and rule over her but her Lord and her King. The church can suffer, but she cannot yield; you may break her confessors alive upon the wheel, but she, in her uprightness, will neither bend nor bow. Neither the best nor the worst of kings or queens may ever dare to put their finger upon the prerogative of Christ as the head of the church. Up, church of God! If once there be any laws of man passed to govern thee, up, dash them in pieces!"[380]

Should a church have a set of governing laws or a constitution?

"When we meet together in church-meeting we cannot make laws for the Lord's kingdom; we dare not attempt it. Such necessary regulations as may be made for carrying out our Lord's commands, to meet for worship, and to proclaim the Gospel, are commendable, because they are acts needful to obedience to His highest laws; but even these minor details are not tolerable if they clearly violate the spirit and mind of Jesus Christ. Law-making in the church was finished in that day when the curse was pronounced on him who should take from or add to the word of God. Christ alone is the legislator of his church—none but He...has left to us his Statute-book, sufficient to guide us in every dilemma."[381] Note: Metropolitan Tabernacle had a constitution, for a member, Charles Noble, referenced it numerous times in a letter to the church after Spurgeon's death.[382]

Church Business

How should the pastor approach the business meeting?

"A pastor who goes to the church-meeting in the spirit of his Master feeling sure that in reliance upon the Holy Spirit he is quite able to answer any untoward spirit, sits at ease, keeps his temper, rises in esteem on each occasion and secures a quiet church; but the unready brother is flurried, probably gets into a passion, commits himself, and inherits a world of sorrow."[383]

What is to be done when committees stall or fail in their work?

"While committees waste their time over resolutions, do something. While Societies and Unions are making constitutions, let us win souls. Too often we discuss and discuss and discuss, while Satan only laughs in his sleeve. It is time we had done planning and sought something to plan."[384]

What is the pastor's role with regard to the overall ministry of the church?

"The minister will do well to supervise all things but interfere with nothing."[385]

Church Members

How might the fears of a new candidate for church membership over meeting with the pastor and review committee be relieved?

"Whenever I hear of candidates being alarmed at coming before our elders or seeing the pastor or making confession of faith before the church, I wish I could say to them: 'Dismiss your fears, beloved ones; we shall be glad to see you, and you will find your intercourse with us a pleasure rather than a trial.' So far from wishing to repel you, if you really do love the Savior, we shall be glad enough to welcome you."[386] (Spurgeon went to the limit to ensure that all who joined the church were regenerated and acceptable. New members were interviewed first by the elders, then by Spurgeon.[387])

What ought the pastor to tell the new church member?

"Dear friend, now that you have become a member of a Christian church, you should say to yourself, 'What can I do for it? I have not come here merely to confess that I am saved, and there to let the matter stop; but I have enlisted in an army that I may be a comrade with other soldiers and be drilled and trained and equipped so that I may know how to march and to go forth to the battle. I have come into the church to be a member of a body. What is my office? Every member has its own special office in the body; it is not there merely for its own comfort, but to be a help to the whole system of which it forms a part. What, then, can I do?' The question which we should each one ask of the Lord is that which Saul asked on the way to Damascus, 'Lord, what wilt thou have me to do?'"[388]

Is it healthy for the preacher to have favorites in the church fellowship?

"Know nothing of parties and cliques, but be the pastor of all the flock, and care for all alike."[389] "It is the extremity of unwisdom for a young man, fresh from college or from another charge, to suffer himself to be earwigged by a clique and to be bribed by kindness and flattery to become a partisan, and so to ruin himself with one-half of his people."[390]

What is the church member's role in foreign missions?

"In looking over a certificate of membership which I had received from a church in New York concerning one of its members who was a sailor, I was pleased to observe that at the back of the certificate there were directions given to the member; and the first one was this: 'You are to remember that as a member of this church going upon a voyage, you are sent by us as a missionary. You are to understand that you and every other member of the church are bound to spread abroad the Savior's name.'"[391]

Church, friendliness, and witness of its members to guests

What is a chief task of the believer at church?

"Every believer should be doubly on the alert in watching for souls. None in that congregation should be able to say, 'We attended that place, but no one spoke to us.'"[392] I always ask my own congregation to preach Christ in the pews. Get hold of the people who come there and tell them about Christ. I know people are a little starched up about the matter sometimes. A little mahogany comes between them and their fellows, but in the church there should be cordiality—the feeling that a man may venture to speak to his neighbor, to say, at least, 'How did you enjoy the sermon?' to start the conversation and detain him for a little while."[393] "I do not think any sermon ought to be preached without each one of you Christian people saying, 'I wonder whether God has blessed the message to this stranger who has been sitting next to me. I will put a gentle question to him and see if I can find out.'"[394]

Commentaries

What is the role of commentaries in the pastor's study?

"True, the Holy Spirit will instruct the seeker, but he works by means. The Ethiopian eunuch might have received divine illumination, and doubtless did receive it, but still, when asked whether he understood the Scripture which he read, he replied, 'How can I unless some man shall guide me?' The guiding man is needed still. Divines who have studied the Scriptures have left us great stores of holy thought which we do well to use. [In *Commenting and Commentaries* he indicates books to acquire and avoid.] Their expositions can never be a substitute for our own meditations, but as water poured down a dry pump often sets it to work to bring up water of its own, so suggestive reading sets the mind in motion on its own account."[395]

What do you say to the preacher that believes all the light he needs is given by the Holy Spirit to him as he studies the Bible by itself?

"It seems odd that certain men who talk so much of what the Holy Spirit reveals to themselves should think so little of what he has revealed to others."[396]

Conflict

What is your advice about the church conflict a pastor inherits?

(Spurgeon's standing rule was not to be a party to disputes that preceded his arrival as pastor at Metropolitan Tabernacle. He states,) "I am quite certain that for my own success and for the prosperity of the church, I took the wisest course by applying my blind eye to all disputes which dated previously to my advent."[397] (Explaining the practice he said,) "Blessed are the peacemakers, and one sure way of peace-making is to let the fire of contention alone. Neither fan it nor stir it nor add fuel to it, but let it go out of itself. Begin your ministry with one blind eye and one deaf ear."[398]

Is it advisable to meddle in the conflicts of other churches?

"I am frequently requested by members of churches to meddle in their home disputes; but unless they come to me with authority, officially appointing me to be umpire, I decline. The person outside the church who interferes in any manner is sure to get the worst of it. Do not consider yourself to be the bishop of all the neighboring churches, but be satisfied with looking after Lystra or Derbe or Thessalonica or whichever church may have been allotted to your care, and leave Philippi and Ephesus in the hands of their own pastors."[399] "My counsel is that we join the 'Knownothings' and never say a word upon a matter till we have heard both sides, and moreover that we do our best to avoid hearing either one side or the other if the matter does not concern us."[400]

Criticism

Have you had to endure criticism from the saints?

"I have suffered enough for one lifetime from those I lived to serve."[401] "You must be able to bear criticism, or you are not fit to be at the head of a congregation."[402]

Deacons and Elders

How important are deacons?

"The church owes an immeasurable debt of gratitude to these men who study her interests day and night, contributing largely of their substance to care for her poor, cheer her ministers, and in every time of trouble as well as prosperity remain faithful at their post."[403]

What should be the pastor's take on deacons?

"If deacons cannot be trusted they ought not to be deacons at all, but if they are worthy of their office, they are worthy of our confidence. I know that instances occur in which they are sadly incompetent and yet they must be borne with, and in such a state of things the pastor must open the eye which otherwise would have remained blind."[404]

"Whatever there may be here and there of mistake, infirmity, and even wrong, we are assured from wide and close observation that the greater number of our deacons are an honor to our faith, and we may style them, as the apostle did his brethren, the 'glory of Christ.'...Deprive the church of her deacons, and she would be bereaved of her most valiant sons;

their loss would be the shaking of the pillars of our spiritual house, and would cause a desolation on every side. Thanks be to God such a calamity is not likely to befall us, for the great Head of the church, in mercy to her, will always raise up a succession of faithful men who will use the office well and earn unto themselves a good degree and much boldness in the faith."[405]

Should the church have elders in addition to deacons?

"There should be both orders of officers [deacons and elders]. The deacons to attend to all secular matters, and the elders to devote themselves to the spiritual part of the work. This division of labor supplies an outlet for two different sorts of talent and allows two kinds of men to be serviceable to the church; and I am sure it is good to have two sets of brethren as officers, instead of one set who have to do everything, and who often are masters of the church instead of the servants, as both deacons and elders should be."[406] (Spurgeon cites biblical reasons for electing elders at Metropolitan Tabernacle in *The Full Harvest* [chapter 5], an autobiography of his life. See Acts 15:2.)

"To our minds, the Scripture seems very explicit as to how this Church should be ordered. We believe that every Church member should have equal rights and privileges, that there is no power in Church officers to execute anything unless they have the full authorization of the members of the Church. We believe, however, that the Church should choose its pastor, and having chosen him, that they should love him and respect him for his work's sake; that with him should be associated the deacons of the Church to take the oversight of pecuniary matters, and the elders of the Church to assist in all the works of the pastorate in the fear of God, being overseers of the flock. Such a Church we believe to be scripturally ordered; and if it abide in the faith, rooted and grounded and settled, such a

Church may expect the benediction of Heaven, and so it shall become the pillar and ground of the truth."[407]

Specifically, what is the duty of elders?

"The seeing of enquirers, the visiting of candidates for church membership, the seeking out of absentees, the caring for the sick and troubled, the conducting of prayer-meetings, catechumen and Bible-classes for the young men—these and other needed offices our brethren the Elders discharge for the church. One Elder is maintained by the church for the especial purpose of visiting our sick poor, and looking after the church-roll, that this may be done regularly and efficiently."[408]

What is the best way to select deacons and elders?

"I have always made it a rule to consult the existing officers of the church before recommending the election of new deacons or elders, and I have also been on the look-out for those who have proved their fitness for office by the work they have accomplished in their private capacity. This plan has worked admirably with us, but other churches have adopted different methods of appointing their officers. In my opinion, the very worst mode of selection is to print the names of all the male members and then vote for a certain number by ballot."[409]

Is there a term limit for deacons and elders?

"In our case, the election of deacons is a permanent one, but the elders are chosen year by year, though they usually continue in their office for life."[410]

Which is the greater office, that of deacon or elder?

"Some will ask the question nowadays: 'Which is the higher office—that of elder or deacon?' and so on. Oh, what triviality! When the Master was going up to Jerusalem to die, there was a contention among the disciples which of them should be the greatest; and so it is with us. At times when grace is low, our opinion of ourselves is very high, and then our love to Christ is little, so that we soon take affront and are quick to resent any little insults, as we think them to be, where perhaps nothing of the kind was meant. Beloved, may we be saved from all this littleness of soul!"[411]

Death

Have you ever pondered what death would be like?

"Well, as a believer in Christ, perhaps I may never come there at all, for there are some that will be alive and remain at the coming of the Son of Man, and these will never die. Then I thought again, *How shall I do in the swelling of Jordan?* I may go through it in the twinkling of an eye. I could envy such a calm departing. Sudden death, sudden glory; taken away in Elijah's chariot of fire with the horses driven at the rate of lightning, so that the spirit scarcely knows that it has left the clay before it sees the brightness of the beatific vision. Well, that may take away some of the alarm of death, the thought that we may not be even a moment in the swelling of Jordan. Then again, I thought, *If I must pass through the swelling of Jordan, yet the real act of death takes no time.* Well, then, as I cannot tell in what physical state I may be when I come to die, I just tried to think again: *How shall I do in the swelling of the Jordan?* I hope I shall do as others have done before me who have built on the same Rock and had the same promises to be their succor. They cried, 'Victory!' So shall I, and after that die quietly and in peace. If the same transporting scene may not be mine, I will at least lay my head upon my Savior's bosom and breathe my life out gently there."[412]

What is the believer's mainstay (assurance and comfort) in dying?

"If the Lord be with us through life, we need not fear for our dying confidence; for when we come to die, we shall find that 'the Lord is there.' Where the billows are most tempestuous and the water is most chill, we shall feel the bottom and know that it is good. Our feet shall stand upon the Rock of Ages when time is passing away. Beloved, from the first of a Christian's life to the last, the only reason why he does not perish is because 'the Lord is there.'"[413]

Deathbed Confession

Are deathbed confessions genuine?

"You know that great fact that a physician once kept a record of a thousand persons who thought they were dying and whom he thought were penitents. He wrote their names down in a book as those who, if they had died, would go to Heaven. They did not die; they lived, and he says that out of the whole thousand he had not three persons who turned out well afterwards, but they returned to their sins again and were as bad as ever. Ah! dear friends, I hope none of you will have such a death-bed repentance as that."[414]

Departure, the preacher

Are there any in God's work who are irreplaceable?

"There's none so important to the Lord's work that the Lord could not replace him by another more efficient."[415]

Depression, the preacher

Do you believe depression is something that many preachers battle?

"As to mental maladies, is any man altogether sane? Are we not all a little off the balance?"[416] "Our work, when earnestly undertaken, lays us open to attacks in the direction of depression. Who can bear the weight of souls without sometimes sinking to the dust?"[417]

Have you experienced depression?

"I have suffered many times from severe sickness and frightful mental depression, sinking almost to despair."[418] "Despondency is not a virtue; I believe it is a vice. I am heartily ashamed of myself for falling into it, but I am sure there is no remedy for it like a holy faith in God."[419]

Did a time ever come when depression was conquered completely?

"I cannot yet call myself free from fits of deep depression…but I am having them less frequently, and therefore I hope they will vanish altogether."[420] (This he stated about five years before his death.)

Doubt

Can people know for sure that they are saved?

"To say, 'I hope so; I trust so' is comfortable, and there are thousands in the fold of Jesus who hardly ever get much further. But to reach the essence of consolation you must say, 'I know.' *If*s, *but*s, and *perhaps*es are sure murderers of peace and comfort. Doubts are dreary things in times of sorrow. Like wasps they sting the soul! If I have any suspicion that Christ is not mine, then there is vinegar mingled with the gall of death. But if I know that Jesus lives for me, then darkness is not dark; even the night is light about me. Surely if Job, in those ages before the coming and advent of Christ, could say, 'I know,' we should not speak less positively."[421]

Education, theological

Why is it that you did not pursue theological education?

[Note: Spurgeon considered college and scheduled an appointment to meet with a college representative. Due to a servant girl's blunder (putting Spurgeon in one waiting room and Dr. Joseph Angus of Stepney's College in another) the two never met. Spurgeon left bitterly disappointed. On the road to Chesterton, he seemed to hear the Lord say, "Seeketh thou great things for thyself? Seek them not." Immediately he forever gave up any thought of attending a theological college. He said,] "I remembered the poor but loving people to whom I ministered and the souls which had been given are in my humble charge; and though I anticipated obscurity and poverty as a result, yet did I then and there renounce the offer of collegiate instruction, determining to remain preaching the Word so long as I had strength to do it."

(That moment in the center of Mid-Summer Common on the road to Chesterton forever impacted the trajectory of his life and ministry. Of that experience, years later, he said,) "From that first day until now, I have acted on no other principle but that of perfect consecration to the work whereunto I am called. I surrendered to my Savior; I gave Him my body, my soul, my spirit…for eternity! I gave Him my talents, my powers, my eyes, my ears…my whole manhood! So far from regretting what I then did, I would fain renew my vows and make them over again."[422]

(Note: Spurgeon believed in theological education and founded the Pastor's College to equip "called" men to preach the Gospel.)

Election

How might the doctrine of election be understood in simplistic terms?

"Leave all curious inquiry about election alone. Go straight to Christ and hide in His wounds, and you shall know your election. The assurance of the Holy Spirit shall be given to you, so that you shall be able to say, 'I know Whom I have believed, and I am persuaded that He is able to keep that which I have committed to Him.' Christ was at the everlasting council; He can tell you whether you were chosen or not. But you cannot find it out in any other way. Go and put your trust in Him, and His answer will be, 'I have loved thee with an everlasting love, therefore with lovingkindness have I drawn thee.' There will be no doubt about His having chosen you when you have chosen Him."[423]

"Lord, call out your elect, and then elect some more."[424]

Encouragement, young preachers

What encouragement might be given to a young preacher who is starting out and is unsure of his potential?

"I was thinking today that next Tuesday (May 3, 1887) it will be just 37 years since I was baptized into the name of the Father and of the Son and of the Holy Spirit! Up to that day, I had never opened my mouth for Christ. I had not even engaged in prayer at a Prayer Meeting, for I was very diffident, and I was afraid to speak of spiritual things! I was not very old, so perhaps my timidity might be excused, but 37 years ago, when I gave myself to Christ, I could not have imagined that I should stand here tonight to preach the Word to these thousands of people. The 'bud' of that day has been 'seed to the sower,' and, blessed be God, it is still 'bread to the eater.' Oh, young men [students at the Pastor's College], you do not know what God can make of you!"[425]

Evangelism

How do you reconcile God's sovereignty with the Great Commission?

"If I see in God's Book two truths which I cannot square with one another, I believe them both."[426]

"Beloved, do your Master's work; win souls; preach Christ; expound your Bibles; pray men to be reconciled to God; plead with men to come to Christ. This kind of work will stand the fire, and when the last great day shall dawn, this will remain to glory and honor."[427]

Evangelists

Do you support vocational evangelists?

(Note: Spurgeon appointed his own evangelists and founded an Evangelist's Association. The Pastor's College had its own Society of Evangelists through which they supported three evangelists. In editions of *The Sword and Trowel* magazine, Spurgeon gave glowing reports of the results of his evangelists.[428])

What did these evangelists believe and preach?

"Their theology is that of the old Puritans. They preach ruin by the Fall; redemption, regeneration, and justification by faith, in the old style and with the old results."[429]

Expository and Topical Sermons

What method of preaching is advisable?

"I am sure that no preaching will last so long, or build up a church so well, as the expository." "The discourse should spring out of the text as a rule. And the more evidently it does so, the better. There must always be a connection, and something more than a remote connection—a real relationship between the sermon and its text."[430] "Although in many cases topical sermons are not only allowable, but very proper, those sermons which expound the exact words of the Holy Spirit are the most useful and the most agreeable to the major part of our congregations."[431]

"We should not unite in any indiscriminate censuring of hortatory addresses, or topical sermons, nor should we agree with the demand that every discourse should be limited to the range of its text, nor even that it should have a text at all; but we should heartily subscribe to the declaration that more expository preaching is greatly needed, and that all preachers would be the better if they were more able expounders of the inspired Word."[432]

Extemporaneous Preaching

Is there a time for extemporaneous preaching?

"It is of no use to rise before an assembly and hope to be inspired upon subjects of which one knows nothing. If anyone is so unwise, the result will be that, as he knows nothing, he will probably say it, and the people will not be edified. But I do not see why a man cannot speak extemporaneously upon a subject that he fully understands. Any tradesman well versed in his line of business could explain it without needing to retire for meditation, and surely I ought to be equally familiar with the first principles of our holy faith. I ought not to feel at a loss when called upon to speak upon topics that constitute the daily bread of my soul."[433] "The power of impromptu speech is invaluable, because it enables a man on the spur of the moment, in an emergency, to deliver himself with propriety. These emergencies will arise."[434]

(With regard to the use of impromptu speech in sermon delivery, Spurgeon said, "The method of unprepared ministrations is practically a failure and theoretically unsound. The Holy Spirit has made no promise to supply spiritual food to the saints by an impromptu ministry."[435])

Failure, pulpit

Have you experienced a feeling of failure after preaching?

"How often have some of us tossed to and fro upon our couch half the night because of conscious shortcomings in our testimony! How frequently have we longed to rush back to the pulpit again to say over again more vehemently what we have uttered in so cold a manner!"[436]

Fear, of ministry

What's the mighty magnet that will enable the preacher's success?

"You fear that you cannot draw a congregation. Try the preaching of a crucified, risen, and ascended Savior; for this is the greatest 'draw' that was ever yet manifested among men. What drew you to Christ but Christ? If you have been drawn to religion by anything else, you will soon be drawn away from it; but Jesus has held you and will hold you even to the end. Why then doubt His power to draw others?"[437]

Foolish Questions

What is your counsel about handling foolish questions?

"Questions upon points wherein Scripture is silent, upon mysteries which belong to God alone, upon prophecies of doubtful interpretation, and upon mere modes of observing human ceremonials are all foolish, and wise men avoid them. Our business is neither to ask nor answer foolish questions, but to avoid them altogether."[438]

Friendliness, of the Pastor

How important is it that the preacher be approachable?

"I love a minister whose face invites me to make him my friend—a man upon whose doorstep you read, 'Salve,' 'Welcome'—and feel that there is no need of that Pompeian warning 'Cave Canem,' 'Beware of the dog.' Give me the man around whom the children come like flies around a honey-pot; they are first-class judges of a good man."[439] "We need to be kind and courteous, for even such a small thing as shaking hands or giving a nod may have an influence."[440]

"No one knows what a smile and a hearty sentence may do. A man who is to do much with men must love them and feel at home with them. When a man has a large, loving heart, men go to him as ships to a haven and feel at peace when they have anchored under the lee of his friendship. Such a man is hearty in private as well as in public; his blood is not cold and fishy, but he is warm as your own fireside."[441]

Fruitfulness

What ought the preacher to expect from the sowing of the Word?

"Do not count all fish that come to the net, or it may happen that your sure disappointment will damp your zeal and diminish your confidence in the Gospel. Expect to take good fish in your net, but reckon upon finding the dog fish there too, breaking your lines and biting your other fish. Out of the best haul a fisherman ever makes there is something to throw away. When you sow good seed, look for wheat to spring up, but be not surprised if tares spring up also."[442]

"The best evidences of the truth of our holy religion are to be found in the marvelous effects it produces. Drunkards, harlots, swearers, thieves, liars, and such like, when reclaimed and regenerated, are the jewels in the crown of the truth; of such we must say in confidence, 'What hath God wrought?' If these fruits were only found united with a learned and eloquent ministry, they would be imputed to the man and not to the truth, but in this case, our enemies themselves are willing witnesses that they cannot so be accounted for."[443]

Fundraising

Is it proper to solicit funding for ministry projects?

(B. R. Wells wrote, "Spurgeon was never afraid to appeal for money, direct deacons of churches to cover students' expenses, or ask for a preaching fee which would be donated to the college."[444] He discovered that it was easier to raise funding for a ministry to children than to train pastors. He said,) "Many will give to an orphanage out of natural compassion who will not contribute to a college out of zeal for the truth."[445]

Gospel, message

What comprises the Gospel?

"Two or three facts constitute the Gospel: "For I delivered unto you first of all that which I also received, how that Christ died for our sins according to the scriptures; And that he was buried, and that he rose again the third day according to the scriptures" (1 Corinthians 15:3–4).[446] "There is no Gospel which has not Christ in it; the modern idea of preaching Truth instead of Christ is a wicked device of Satan."[447]

Gossip

How should the pastor handle gossipers?

"Let the creatures buzz, and do not even hear them, unless indeed they buzz so much concerning one person that the matter threatens to be serious; then it will be well to bring them to book and talk in sober earnestness to them. Assure them that you are obliged to have facts definitely before you, that your memory is not very tenacious, that you have many things to think of, that you are always afraid of making any mistake in such matters, and that if they would be good enough to write down what they have to say the case would be more fully before you, and you could give more time to its consideration."[448]

Growth, church

How did you get the great congregation at Metropolitan Tabernacle?

"Somebody asked me how I got my congregation. I never got it at all. I did not think it my business to do so but only to preach the Gospel. Why, my congregation got my congregation."[449]

Healing

What is your view of the use of medicines to provide healing?

"You know all healing power is from God; whatever healing properties there may be in vegetable or mineral substances [medicines], He, with gracious forethought, put them there, while the ability to rightly use them is equally His gift. I like what a French surgeon had sculptured on his college gate: 'I dress the wounds, and God healed him.'"[450]

Heathen, will they be saved

Will the heathen be saved if no one takes them the Gospel?

"I remember one who spoke on the missionary question one day saying, 'The great question is not whether the heathen be saved if we do not send them the Gospel, but are we saved ourselves if we do not send them the Gospel?'"[451]

Heaven

How is Heaven like unto a barn for believers?

"Every hour the saints are being gathered into the barn. That is where they want to be. We feel no pain at the news of ingathering, for we wish to be safely stored up by our Lord. If the wheat that is in the field could speak, every ear would say, 'The ultimatum for which we are living and growing is the barn, the granary.' Every process with the wheat is tending towards the granary. So is it with us: everything is working toward Heaven, toward the gathering place, toward the congregation of the righteous, toward the vision of our Redeemer's face. Our death will cause no jar in our life-music; it will involve no pause or even discord; it is part of a program, the crowning of our whole history. I delight to think of Heaven as His barn."[452]

How far away is Heaven?

"The distance between the glorified spirits in Heaven and the militant saints on earth seems great, but it is not so. We are not far from home. Heaven…is just one sigh and we get there.

Our departed friends are only in the upper room, as it were, of the same house; they have not gone far off; they are upstairs, and we are down below."[453]

Hell

Do you believe in the eternal damnation of the unsaved?

"While I believe in eternal punishment, and must do or throw away my Bible, I also believe that God will give to the lost every consideration consistent with His love. There is nothing vindictive in Him, nor can there be in His punishment of the ungodly."[454]

Is the fire in Hell real?

"Now, do not begin telling me that is metaphorical fire; who cares for that? If a man were to threaten to give me a metaphorical blow on the head, I should care very little about it; he would be welcome to give me as many as he pleased. And what say the wicked? 'We do not care about metaphorical fires.' But they are real, sir—yes, as real as yourself. There is a real fire in Hell, as truly as you now have a real body—a fire exactly like that which we have on earth in everything except this, that it will not consume, though it will torture you."[455]

Holiness, the minister

What is the foundational imperative of being useful in God's work?

"God make us holy; sanctify us, spirit, soul, and body, and then we shall be made finely serviceable both to the Church and to the world."[456] "Unless our faith makes us pine after holiness, it is no better than the faith of devils, and perhaps it is not even so good as that. A holy man is the workmanship of the Holy Spirit."[457]

Holy Spirit

In what way doth the Holy Spirit teach the believer?

"The Holy Spirit teaches us in three ways: suggestion, direction, and illumination. There are thoughts that dwell in our minds that are suggestions put there by the Spirit for us to follow. Sometimes He leads us by direction, leading our thoughts along into a more excellent channel than that which we started. Sometimes He leads us by illuminating the Word of God to us."[458]

Humor, in preaching

Is humor appropriate in the pulpit?

"If occasionally I make you smile, I do not mind, because sometimes I can get the truth into your heart that way when I cannot get it in any other way."[459] (To a person that objected to a humorous expression Spurgeon used in a sermon, he replied,) "If you had known how many others I kept back, you would not have found fault with that one, but you would have commended me for the restraint I had exercised."[460] (Further he said that only in the presence of God would it be revealed the number of people that first were lured to the Gospel by a joke or anecdote, which was like bait to the fish concealing the hook on which they were joyously caught.[461])

"The twelfth commandment is 'Thou shalt pull a long face on Sunday.' I must confess that I would rather hear people laugh than I would see them sleep in the house of God; and I would rather get the truth into them through the medium of ridicule than I would have it neglected, or leave the people to perish through lack of reception of the message."[462]

Illustrations and Antidotes

What value are sermonic illustrations?

"No reason exists why the preaching of the Gospel should be a miserable operation either to the speaker or to the hearer. Pleasantly profitable let all our sermons be. A house must not have thick walls without openings; neither must a discourse be all made up of solid slabs of doctrine without a window of comparison or a lattice of poetry; if so, our hearers will gradually forsake us."[463] "Our congregations hear us with pleasure when we give them a fair measure of imagery; when an anecdote is being told, they rest, take a breath, and give play to their imaginations, and thus prepare themselves for the sterner work which lies before them in listening to our profounder expositions."[464]

How do you get sermonic illustrations?

"Whenever I have been permitted sufficient respite from my ministerial duties to enjoy a lengthened tour, or even a short excursion, I have been in the habit of carrying with me a small notebook in which I have jotted down any illustrations which have occurred to me by the way. My recreations have been all the more pleasant because I have made them subservient to my life-work. The notebook has been useful in my travels as a mental purse. If not fixed upon paper, ideas are apt to vanish with the occasion which suggested them. A word or two will suffice to bring an incident or train of thought to remembrance; and therefore, it would be inexcusable in a minister, who needs so much, not to preserve all that comes in his way. From the pencil marks of the pocketbook, my notes have been enlarged into more permanent manuscript and have been of great service to me. Out of hundreds of metaphors and anecdotes thus collected, I have used the main body in my constant sermonizing."[465]

What is your caution about the use of illustrations?

"Illustrate, by all means, but do not let the sermon be all illustrations, or it will be only suitable for an assembly of simpletons."[466]

Impromptu sermons

Some men think that the Holy Spirit will enable their speaking without preparation. What saith you?

"The method of unprepared ministrations is practically a failure and theoretically unsound. Unstudied thoughts coming from the mind without previous research, without the subjects in hand having been investigated at all, must be of a very inferior quality, even from the most superior men. The Holy Spirit has made no promise to supply spiritual food for the saints by an impromptu ministry. If we can study and do not, if we can have a studious ministry and will not, we have no right to call in a divine agent to make up the deficits of our idleness or eccentricity."[467]

Infants, baptism

Is infant baptism biblical?

"We cannot but regard infant baptism as unscriptural, and to everything that is unscriptural we, as disciples of Jesus Christ, must be opposed."[468]

Infants, salvation

Are infants that die saved?

(An inquirer in correspondent dated June 12, 1869, asked Spurgeon if he ever stated, "There is in Hell infants a span long." He replied,) "I have never at any time in my life said, believed, or imagined that an infant under any circumstances would be cast into Hell. I have always believed in the salvation of all infants."[469]

How are they saved then?

"By works? No, for they have never worked! By their natural innocence? No, for if that innocence could have admitted them to Heaven, it must also have sufficed to save them from pain and death. We know little of the matter, but we suppose them to undergo regeneration before they enter Heaven, for that which is born of the flesh is flesh, and to enter the spiritual world, they must be born of the Spirit. But whatever is worked in them, it is clear that they do not enter the kingdom by the force of intellect or will or merit, but as a matter of Free Grace, having no reference to anything that they have done or have felt!"[470]

Laborers, the harvest

What biblical text weighs on your heart the heaviest?

"This text [Matthew 9:38] is laid on my heart. It lies more on my heart than any other in the Bible. It is one that haunts me perpetually and has done for many years."[471] "We want laborers, not loiterers. We need men on fire, and I beseech you, pray to God to send them. The harvest can never be reaped by men who will not labor. They must off with their coats and go at it in their shirtsleeves. I mean they must doff their dignities and get to Christ's work as if they meant it, like real harvest men. They must sweat at their work, for nothing in the harvest field can be done without the sweat of the face, or in the pulpit without the sweat of the soul."[472]

Law, the Ten Commandments

What role doth the Law play in man's salvation?

"The law is the needle, and you cannot draw the silken thread of the Gospel through a man's heart unless you first send the needle of the law to make way for it. If men do not understand the law, they will not feel that they are sinners."[473]

Lord's Supper, communion

How often should the Lord's Supper be observed?

"I do trust, dear friends, that in a very short time we shall celebrate the Lord's Supper every Sabbath day."[474] "It seems to me that the Lord's Supper should be received by us often. When the apostle says in our text, 'As often as ye eat this bread, and drink this cup,' and our Lord said in instituting the ordinance, 'This do ye, as oft as ye drink it, in remembrance of Me,' I will not say that their words absolutely teach that we should frequently come to the table of communion; but I do think they give us a hint that if we act rightly, we shall often observe this supper of the Lord. If there be any rule as to the time for the observance of this ordinance, it surely is every Lord's Day. At any rate, let it be often."[475] "We must keep on gathering at His table, giving thanks, breaking bread, and proclaiming His death till the trump of the archangel shall startle us—and then we shall feel it to be truly blessed to be found obediently remembering Him when he puts in His appearance at the last."[476]

"Shame on the Christian church that she put it off to once a month and mar the first day of the week by depriving it of its glory in the meeting together for fellowship and breaking of bread and showing forth the death of Christ till he comes. They who once know the sweetness of each Lord's Day celebrating His supper, will not be content, I am sure, to put it off to less frequent seasons."[477]

(In the autobiography of Spurgeon's life by his wife and secretary it states,) "[I have] long held and taught that the apostolic precedents all appeared to indicate that the celebration of the sacred supper should take place each Lord's Day, and therefore, whether at home or abroad, [I] always attended the communion every Sabbath if it was possible."[478] "I love to come every Lord's Day to the communion table; I should be very sorry to come only once a month, or, as some do, only once a year. I could not afford to come as seldom as that. I need to be reminded, forcibly reminded, of my dear Lord and Master very often."[479]

Do the elements literally change into the body and blood of Christ in the Lord's Supper observance?

"Notice that it is bread that they eat, and it is wine that they drink; nothing is said about transubstantiation here; but 'as often as ye eat this bread'—and it is bread and nothing but bread—'and drink this cup,' which still remains but a cup and its contents just what they were before—'ye do shew the Lord's death till he come.'"[480]

Who may partake of the Lord's Supper?

"We do not hold it right to admit all persons indiscriminately to the Lord's Supper; we believe the Lord's table is the place of communion, and we would have none there with whom we cannot have true Christian fellowship. We feel that we cannot commune with them. We hold it to be our bounden duty, as God hath given us authority in His Church, to prevent those from drawing nigh unto the table who would but commune unworthily and so eat and drink unto themselves judgment, as the word in the 29th verse [1 Corinthians 11] should be translated. Among our Baptist churches, fashioned, we trust, somewhat nearer to the Scriptural order than certain others we wot of, we do exercise at least some measure of discipline. We require from those who are members of the church and who are, by reason of that membership, entitled to commune, that they should, at their reception, give us what we consider satisfactory proofs of their conversion; and we require of them afterwards that their conduct should be consistent with the law of Christ; otherwise, we should not in the first place receive them, or having received them, it should not be long before, by the Scriptural process of excommunication, we should remove from our midst those members whose lives and conversation were not in accordance with the Gospel of our Lord and Savior Jesus Christ."[481]

Manipulation, the invitation

What about the danger of manipulation in the invitation?

"It very often happens that the converts that are born in excitement die when the excitement is over....Some of the most glaring sinners known to me were once members of a church and were, as I believe, led to make a profession by *undue* pressure, well-meant but ill-judged."[482]

Manuscript, sermon

Should I preach from a manuscript?

"Leave them at home afterwards, but still write them out, that you may be preserved from a slipshod style."[483]

What notes do you take into the pulpit?

"I am guided to the best form of outline, which I copy out on a half sheet of notepaper for use in the pulpit."[484]

Missions

Did you consider being a missionary?

"I have made it a solemn question whether I might not testify in China or India the grace of Jesus, and in the sight of God I have answered it. I solemnly feel that my position in England will not permit my leaving the sphere in which I now am, or else tomorrow I would offer myself as a missionary."[485]

Does Metropolitan Tabernacle send support to foreign missionaries?

(The church and college supported work in China, India, Africa, and other places.)

Music, worship services

Is instrumental music allowable in the church?

(At the Tabernacle, hymns were sung without musical accompaniment. W. Y. Fullerton asserts, "Spurgeon had a rooted objection to instrumental music in the worship of God. But he came at length to tolerate an American organ in mission services, and he made Manton Smith a present of a silver cornet on which was inscribed the text from the ninety-eighth Psalm, 'With trumpets and sound of cornet make a joyful noise before the LORD, the King.' Once when asked his opinion of a grand organ, he answered, 'Yes, it praises its maker very well.' He also disliked choirs and detested anthems. After a special musical performance, he was told that one of the pieces was supposed to have been sung by David. 'Then I know why Saul threw his javelin at him,' he replied, much to the chagrin of the choirmaster."[486])

Pastor

Who is the pastor?

"The true shepherd spirit is an amalgam of many precious graces. He is hot with zeal, but he is not fiery with passion. He is gentle, and yet he rules his class. He is loving, but he does not wink at sin. He has power over the lambs, but he is not domineering or sharp. He has cheerfulness, but not levity; freedom, but not license; solemnity, but not gloom."[487] "As is the workman, such will the work be."[488] "Ministers are servants: they are not guests, but waiters; not landlords, but laborers."[489] "Some ministers need to be told that they are the same species as their hearers."[490]

What is the most essential character trait of the minister?

"He [the preacher] is not sent into the world to be a hermit or a monk. It is not his vocation to stand on a pillar all day, above his fellowmen like that hair-brained Simon Stylites of olden time. You are not to warble from the top of a tree like an invisible nightingale, but to be a man among men, saying to them, 'I also am as you are in all that relates to man.' Salt is of no use in the box; it must be rubbed into the meat, and our personal influence must penetrate and season society. Keep aloof from others, and how can you benefit them? Our Master went to a wedding and ate bread with publicans and sinners."[491] "You must love the people and mix with them if you are to be of service to them. There are some ministers who really are much better men than others, yet they do not accomplish so much good as those who are more human, those who go and sit down with the people."[492]

What man poses the greatest danger to the preacher?

"Beware of no man more than of yourself; we carry our worst enemies within us."[493]

Is the ordination of a minister necessary?

"Is not the Divine call the real ordination to preach, and the call of the church the only ordination to the pastorate? The church is competent, under the guidance of the Holy Spirit, to do her own work....Is there then a ritual? Are we as much bound by an unwritten extempore liturgy as others by the Book of Common Prayer? Must there always be 'usual questions'? And why 'usual'? Is there some legendary rule for the address to the church and the address to the pastor? I do not object to any one of these things, but I do question the propriety of stereotyping them and speaking of the whole affair as if it were a matter to gone about according to a certain pattern seen in the holy mount, or an order given forth in trust to the saints."[494] (Spurgeon never was ordained by man.)

Is it advisable for a church to call a young man to be their pastor?

"One of the best things that a church can do is to catch a minister young and train him for themselves. Some of the happiest and longest pastorates in our denomination commenced with the invitation of a young man from the country to a post for which he was barely qualified. His mistakes were borne with, his efforts were encouraged, and he grew; and the church grew with him. His pastorate continued for many a year since he was under no temptation to leave for another position, because he felt at home and could say, like one of old, 'I dwell among mine own people.'"[495] (Obviously, he was one of those young men.)

What counsel do you give him who is contemplating the ministry?

"If you think you can never honor Christ till you enter a pulpit, it may be just possible that you will afterwards honor Him best by getting out of it as quickly as you can."[496]

Pastor, prayer

How important is pastoral prayer in the worship service?

"I am not able to see any reason for depriving me of the holiest, sweetest, and most profitable exercise which my Lord has allotted me; if I have my choice, I will sooner yield up the sermon than the [pastoral] prayer."[497] (Dinsdale T. Young, who heard Spurgeon's pulpit prayers, often said, "Never did I hear him pray without adoringly saying, 'Lord, it is good for us to be here.'"[498] Further, he said, "Spurgeon always pleaded for the immediate moment. 'Now' was his plea, and verily then and there all were blessed of God.")

Who should say the prayer?

"As a rule, if called upon to preach, conduct the prayer yourself."[499]

How might the pastoral prayer be most effective?

"As to our prayers in public, let it never be truthfully said that they are official, formal, and cold; yet they will be so if the supply of the Spirit be scant."[500] "Let your prayers be earnest, full of fire, vehemence, prevalence. I pray the Holy Ghost to instruct every student of [our] College so to offer public prayer, that God shall always be served of his best. Let your petitions be plain and heart-felt; and while your people may sometimes feel that the sermon was below the mark, may they also feel that the prayer compensated for all."[501] "Proper preparation means solemn consideration beforehand of the importance of prayer, meditation upon the needs of men's souls, and a remembrance of the promises which we are to plead, and thus coming before the Lord with a petition written upon the fleshly tables of the heart. This is surely better than coming to God at random, rushing before the throne at haphazard without a definite error or desire....Seeds of prayer thus sown in the memory will yield a constant golden harvest, as the Spirit shall warm your soul with hallowed fire in the hour of the congregational prayer."[502]

What caution might you give the pastor regarding pastoral prayer?

"Beware of having an eye to the auditors; beware of becoming rhetorical to please the listeners. Prayer must not be transformed into an 'oblique sermon.' It is little short of blasphemy to make devotion an occasion for display.... Remember the people in your prayers, but do not mold your supplications to win their esteem....Preach in the sermon and pray in the prayer."[503]

Pastor, unpardonable presumption

What is the preacher's unpardonable presumption?

"Habitually to come into the pulpit unprepared is unpardonable presumption; nothing can more effectually lower ourselves and our office."[504] "He who no longer sows in the study will no more reap in the pulpit."[505] (My Bible college professor Wallace Rogers said, "If you're too busy to study, then you're too busy.") "To us ministers the maintenance of our power in the pulpit should be our great concern; we must occupy that spiritual watchtower with our hearts and minds awake and in full vigor. It will not avail us to be laborious pastors if we are not earnest preachers."[506] "Spread your sail, but remember what you sometimes sing, 'I can only spread the sail; Thou! must breathe the auspicious gale.' Only be sure you have the sail up. Do not miss the gale for want of

---

Your pulpit preparations are your first business, and if you neglect these, you will bring no credit upon yourself or your office. I have no belief in that ministry which ignores laborious preparation.

Charles Spurgeon

---

preparation."[507]

"Your pulpit preparations are your first business, and if you neglect these, you will bring no credit upon yourself or your office. Bees are making honey from morning till night, and we should be always gathering stores for our people. I have no belief in that ministry which ignores laborious preparation."[508]

Pastoral, work

What kind of work is the pastor engaged in?

"Ours is more than mental work—it is heart work, the labor of our inmost soul."[509]

What things impact the pastor's work?

"Our work is, no doubt, greatly affected, for good or evil, by the condition of the congregation, the condition of the church, and the condition of the deacons."[510]

What is the preacher's top priority in the pastorate?

"I recommend every young minister to make his pulpit his first business. Your people may grumble that you don't go about and drink as many cups of tea [coffee] at their houses as they would like. If you give them good food on the Sabbath, they will put up with a great deal."[511]

What is the pastor to do when he doesn't feel up to the task?

"If we never do any work for Christ except when we feel up to the mark, we shall not do much. We must be always at it until we wear ourselves out, throwing our whole soul into the work in all weather for Christ's sake."[512]

Persecution

Is persecution to be expected by the preacher?

"Every David has his Saul, every Nehemiah his Sanballat, and every Mordecai his Haman."[513]

Persistence, preaching

Preaching requires patience and persistence. What audience demands both the most?

"What a forgetful generation do most preachers address! Alas, many of our hearers must have the Gospel preached to them again and again and again till the preacher is well-near weary with his hopeless task! They are like men who see their natural faces in a glass and go their way to forget what manner of men they are. They still live in sin. The Word has no abiding place in their hearts."[514]

Planned Preaching

What about planned preaching?

"I am obliged to owe a great deal of my strength to variety rather than to profundity. It is questionable whether the great majority of list preachers had not better burn their programs if they would succeed!"[515]

"Ordinarily, and for ordinary men, it seems to me that pre-arranged discourses are a mistake. Surely to go through a long epistle must require a great deal of genius in the preacher and demand a world of patience on the part of the hearers. I am moved by a yet deeper consideration in what I have now said: it strikes me that many a truly living, earnest preacher would feel a program to be a fetter. Should the preacher announce for next Lord's Day a topic full of joy, requiring liveliness and exaltation of spirit, it is very possible that he may, from various causes, find himself in a sad and burdened state of mind; nevertheless, he must put the new wine into his old bottle and go up to the wedding feast wearing his sackcloth and ashes, and worst of all, this he may be bound to repeat for a whole month. Is this quite as it should be? It is important that the speaker should be in tune with his theme, but how is this to be secured unless the election of the topic is left to influences which shall work at the time? A man is not a steam engine, to run on metals, and it is unwise to fix him in one groove. Very much of the preacher's power will lie in his whole soul being in accord with the subject, and I should be afraid to appoint a subject for a certain date, lest when the time come, I should not be in the key for it. Besides, it is not easy to see how a man can exhibit dependence upon the guidance of the Spirit of God when he has already prescribed his own route. Even so will our sermons come to us, fresh from Heaven, when required. I am jealous of anything which should hinder your daily dependence upon the Holy Spirit, and therefore I register the opinion already given."[516]

Poisoned Arrows

How might we face the poisoned arrows of slander, ridicule, falsehood and demeaning insinuation?

"The Lord God promises us that if we cannot silence them, we shall, at least, escape from being ruined by them. They condemn us for the moment, but we shall condemn them at last and forever. The mouth of them that speak lies shall be stopped, and their falsehoods shall be turned to the honor of those good men who suffered by them."[517]

Politics

Should religion be brought into politics?

"I often hear it said, 'Do not bring religion into politics.' This is precisely where it ought to be brought! I would have the Cabinet and Members of Parliament do the work of the nation as before the Lord, and I would have the nation, either in making war or peace, consider the matter by the light of righteousness. We have had enough of clever men without conscience. Now let us see what honest, God-fearing men will do."[518]

Ought the preacher's sermons to be political?

"In proportion as the preaching becomes political and the pastor sinks the spiritual in the temporal, strength is lost and not gained."[519] "Take the eighteen volumes of the *Metropolitan Tabernacle Pulpit* (at the time only 18 volumes had been published), and see if you can find eighteen pages of matter which even look towards politics; nay, more, see if there be one solitary sentence concerning politics which did not, to the preacher's mind, appear to arise out of his text or to flow from the natural run of his subject."[520] "The truth is that many of us are loath to touch politics at all and would never do so if we were not driven to it. Our life-theme is the Gospel, and to deal with the sins of the State is our 'strange work,' which we only enter upon under the solemn constraints of duty."[521]

"For a Christian minister to be an active partisan of Whigs or Tories, busy in canvassing and eloquent at public meetings for rival factions, would be of ill repute. For the Christian to forget his heavenly citizenship and occupy himself about the objects of place-hunters would be degrading to his high calling, but there are points of inevitable contact between the higher and lower spheres, points where politics persist in coming into collision with our faith, and there we shall be traitors both to Heaven and earth if we consult our comfort by sinking into the rear."[522]

(Spurgeon arrived late to preach for his friend John Offord and apologized, explaining the tardiness was due to a block on the road and stopping to vote with his father. "To vote!" exclaimed the good man; "but, my dear brother, I thought you were a citizen of the New Jerusalem!"

"So I am," replied Mr. Spurgeon, "but my 'old man' is a Citizen of this world."

"Ah! but you should mortify your 'old man.'"

"That is exactly what I did; for my 'old man' is a Tory, and I made him vote for the Liberals!"[523])

Praise, of man

What caution is needful about the praise of man?

"Play the man, and do not demean yourself by seeking compliments like little children when dressed in new clothes."[524] "Who are we, that we should receive praise where Jesus received spittle?"[525]

Prayer, its frequency

How often should the pastor pray?

"Regular retirement is to be maintained, but continued communion with God is to be our aim. As a rule, we ministers ought never to be many minutes without actually lifting up our hearts in prayer."[526]

"Prayer pulls the rope below, and the great bell rings above in the ears of God. Some scarcely stir the bell, for they pray so languidly. Others give but an occasional pluck at the rope. But he who wins with Heaven is the man who grasps the rope boldly and pulls continuously, with all his might."[527]

Prayer, Spurgeon's final

What will you pray for at death's door?

"If there is only one prayer which I might pray before I died, it should be this: 'Lord, send thy church men filled with the Holy Ghost and with fire.'"[528]

Prayer Meeting

Should the weekly prayer meeting be maintained?

"Somehow we must keep up the prayer meetings, for they are at the very secret source of power with God and with men."[529]

"Keep up the prayer meeting, whatever else flags; it is the great business [meeting] of the week, the best service between the Sabbaths." (Spurgeon's autobiography states of the Monday night prayer meeting: "The whole spirit of the gathering made it a source of peculiar helpfulness to all who were in constant attendance, while occasional visitors carried away with them even to distant lands influences and impulses which they never wished to lose or to forget."[530])

"Thomas would not believe that his Lord was risen. Why? Because he was not at the last prayer meeting; for we are told that Thomas was not there. And those who are often away from devotional meetings are very apt to have doubting frames."[531]

Preaching

What is true preaching?

"I am determined, as far as ever I can, to preach the Gospel plainly and simply, so that everybody may understand it."[532] "We have a fixed faith to preach, my brethren, and we are sent forth with a definite message from God. We are not let to fabricate the message as we go along. We are not sent forth by our Master with a general commission arranged on this fashion: 'As you shall think in your heart and invent in your head, so preach. Keep abreast of the times. Whatever the people want to hear, tell them that, and they shall be saved.' Verily, we read not so. There is something definite in the Bible. It is not quite a lump of wax to be shaped at our will, or a roll or cloth to be cut according to the prevailing fashion. We stand in a very solemn position, and ours should be the spirit of old Micaiah, who said, 'As the Lord my God liveth, before whom I stand, whatsoever the Lord saith unto me that will I speak.' Neither less nor more than God's Word are we called to state, but that Word we are bound to declare in a spirit which convinces the sons of men that, whatever they may think of it, we believe God and are not to be shaken in our confidence in Him."[533] "Woe unto us if we dare to speak the Word of the Lord with less than our whole heart and soul and strength. Woe unto us if we handle the Word as if it were an occasion for display!"[534]

Preparation, preaching

What is the secret to effectual preaching?

"Endeavor to keep the matter of your sermonizing as fresh as you can. With abundant themes diligently illustrated by fresh metaphors and experiences, we shall not weary, but under God's hand shall win our hearers' ears and hearts."[535]

"The law goes first, like the needle, and draws the Gospel thread after it; therefore, preach concerning sin, righteousness, and judgment to come."[536] "If any one note is dropped from the divine harmony of truth, the music may be sadly marred. Your people may fall into grave spiritual diseases through the lack of a certain form of spiritual nutriment which can only be supplied by the doctrines which you withhold."[537] "My brethren, the preaching of the gospel minister should always have soulwinning for its object. I have felt as though I could weep tears of blood that the time of the congregation on the Sabbath should be wasted by listening to wordy rhetoric, when what was wanted was a plain, urgent pleading with men's hearts and consciences."[538]

(Spurgeon would have liked W. A. Criswell's bottom line about preaching: "So God's messenger may say today, 'I wasn't wrapped in my own academic robes on the Lord's Day. I wasn't hiding behind all the degrees that I have tried to win on the Lord's Day. I wasn't trying to say what man would say on the Lord's Day. I was in the Spirit on the Lord's Day. When I walked into the pulpit, it might have been "pore" English, faulty construction, and homiletically unsound; but when I stood there, such as I was, and what I could do, that did I say and preach in the power of the Holy Spirit. I was in the Spirit on the Lord's Day. Then, as I tried to speak and to preach and to shepherd my people, I did it in the unction and power and baptism of the Holy Spirit, so help me God.'"[539]

How much training does a preacher need to preach?

(Spurgeon gives answer by quoting Joshua Shute: "That the sermon has most learning in it that has most plainness. Hence it is the great scholar was wont to say, 'Lord, give me learning enough that I may preach plain enough.'"[540])

Projects, undertaking

What is the determinative factor in moving forward with a new project?

"Some of our brethren have asked [when the new Tabernacle was yet unfinished], 'When Mr. Spurgeon dies, who will take his place?'—as if God could not raise up servants when He would, or as if we ought to neglect our present duty because of something which may happen in fifty years' time. You say, perhaps, 'You give yourself a long lease—fifty years.' I don't know why I should not have it; it may come to pass, and will, if the Lord has so ordained....I was nineteen when I was invited; and is it not possible that I also, by Divine grace, may serve my generation for a long period of time? At any rate, when I am proposing to commence a plan, I never think about whether I shall live to see it finished, for I am certain that, if it is God's plan, He will surely finish it, even if I should have to leave the work undone."[541]

Reading

Is reading a priority for ministers?

"You may get much instruction from books which afterwards you may use as a true weapon in your Lord and Master's service."[542] "Master those books you have. Read them thoroughly. Bathe in them until they saturate you. Read and reread them....Digest them. Let them go into your very self. Peruse a good book several times and make notes and analyses of it. A student will find that his mental constitution is more affected by one book thoroughly mastered than by twenty books he has merely skimmed. Little learning and much pride comes from hasty reading. Some men are disabled from thinking by their putting meditation away for the sake of much reading. In reading, let your motto be 'much not many.'"[543]

"'Give attendance to reading.' If, brethren, you would bless God's Church and train up a band of really intelligent Christians, do not be always appealing to the emotions only, but give out also good, sound, strong gospel doctrine, and illustrate the doctrine so as to expound and commend to others. Do this especially by reading the words of the greatest masters in Scripture theology, and these will prove your delightful and dear companions and your splendid helpers in making your ministry richly profitable to your hearers."[544]

(Spurgeon says about Paul's books,) "[Paul] is inspired, and yet he wants books! He has been preaching at least for thirty years, and yet he wants books! He had seen the Lord, and yet he wants books! He had had a wider experience than most men, and yet he wants books! He had been caught up into the third heaven and had heard things which it was unlawful for a man to utter, yet he wants books! He had written the major part of the New Testament, and yet he wants books!...Paul cries, 'Bring the books'—join in the cry."[545]

(Spurgeon practiced what he preached by reading six books weekly despite the strenuous schedule.)

What should the pastor read?

"Renounce as much as you will all light literature, but study as much as possible sound theological works, especially the Puritanic writers and expositions of the Bible."[546] "Read the books, by all manner of means, but…especially stand fast by that Book which is infallible."[547]

(Spurgeon advised Charles in a letter from Mentone,) "Stick to your studies. Read *Matthew Henry* right through, if you can, before you are married; for after that event, I fear that Jacob may supplant him."[548] (It was Spurgeon's habit with a thoroughly bad book, morally or doctrinally, to tear it into little pieces or to thrust it into the fire to insure it would do no harm to anyone.[549])

What is your chief book?

"I should like always to be reading my Bible."[550] "Now, it must be 'especially the parchments' [2 Timothy 4:13] with all our reading; let it be especially the Bible. Persons read the views of their denominations as set forth in the periodicals, they read the views of their leader as set forth in his sermons or his works, but the Book, the good old Book, the divine fountainhead from which all revelation wells up—this is too often left. You may go to human puddles until you forsake the clear crystal stream which flows from the throne of God. Read the books, but especially the parchments.…Stand fast by that Book which is infallible, the revelation of our Lord and Savior Jesus Christ."[551]

Regret, the preacher's

What do you think will be a great regret of the preacher?

"If I had only one more sermon to preach before I died, I know what it would be about. It should be about my Lord Jesus Christ; and I think that when we get to the end of our ministry, one of our greatest regrets will be that we did not preach more of Him."[552]

Reputation, Spurgeon's

How do you think history will write of you?

"However much I may now be misrepresented, it will one day be known that I have honestly striven for the glory of my Master."[553] "'Let the wicked say what they will of me,' said the apostle; 'I commit my character to the Judge of the quick and dead.'"[554]

Resignation and Retirement

How ought the minister to feel upon resignation or retirement from a church?

"When Latimer resigned his bishopric, Foxe tells us that as he put off his rochet from his shoulders, he gave a skip on the floor for joy, 'feeling his shoulders so light at being discharged of such a burden.' To be relieved of our wealth or high position is to be unloaded of weighty responsibilities and should not cause us to fret, but rather to rejoice as those who are lightened of a great load. If we cease from office in the church, or from public honors, or from power of any sort, we may be consoled by the thought that there is just so much the less for us to answer for at the great audit, when we must give an account of our stewardship."[555]

At the close of life, what would you like to do?

"I would like to rise from my bed during the last five minutes of my life to bear witness to the Divine sacrifice and the sin-atoning blood. I would then repeat those words which speak the truth of substitution most positively, even should I shock my hearers; for how could I regret that as in Heaven my first words would be to ascribe my salvation to my Master's blood, my last act on earth was to shock His enemies by a testimony to the same fact?"[556]

Restoration, the pastor

Is a probationary period advisable for preachers that fall into open sin?

"How many that flamed like comets in the sky of the religious world have been quenched in darkness!"[557] "The highest moral character must be sedulously maintained. I question, gravely question whether a man who has grossly sinned should be very readily restored to the pulpit. As John Angell James remarks, 'When a preacher of righteousness has stood in the way of sinners, he should never again open his lips in the great congregation until his repentance is as notorious as his sin.' Let those who have been shorn by the sons of Ammon tarry at Jericho till their beards be grown. [This] is an accurate enough metaphor for dishonored and characterless men."[558] (Let the preacher that falters gravely) "go into seclusion for a while until [your] character [has] been to some extent restored."[559]

Revivals and Evangelistic Services

What about the use of evangelists and fellow pastors?

"To call in another brother every now and then to take the lead in evangelistic services will be found very wise and useful, for there are some fish that never will be taken in your net but will surely fall to the lot of another fisherman. Fresh voices penetrate where the accustomed sound has lost effect, and they tend also to beget a deeper interest in those already attentive. Sound and prudent evangelists may lend help even to the most efficient pastor and gather in fruit which he has failed to reach; at any rate it makes a break in the continuity of ordinary services and renders them less likely to become monotonous. Never suffer jealousy to hinder you in this."[560]

When is a revival in the church needed?

"A sad decline of the vitality of godliness, the absence of sound doctrine, and want of downright earnestness in its members."[561]

What is the best way to prepare for a revival?

"Christian men should never speak of 'getting up a revival.' Where are you going to get it up from? I do not know any place from which you can get it up. We must bring revival down if it is to be worth having. We must enquire of the Lord to do it for us. Too often the temptation is to enquire for an eminent revivalist or ask whether a great preacher could be induced to come. Now I do not object to inviting soul-winning preachers or to any other plans of usefulness, but our main business is to enquire of the Lord, for, after all, He alone can give the increase."[562]

"There are instrumental causes; and the main instrumental cause of a great revival must be the bold, faithful, fearless preaching of the truth as it is in Jesus."[563]

Are evangelistic meetings effective?

"We had notable evangelists among us preaching the Gospel, and some persons imagined that when they were gone, we should see no more of the work, but it is not so; sinners are still coming to Jesus, and they will come."[564]

Rules, to live by

Should a minister make a list of rules to govern life?

"I have found, in my own spiritual life, that the more rules I lay down for myself, the more sins I commit. The habit of regular morning and evening prayer is one which is indispensable to a believer's life, but the prescribing of the length of prayer, and the constrained remembrance of so many persons and subjects, may gender unto bondage and strangle prayer rather than assist it. To say I will humble myself at such a time and rejoice at such another season is nearly as much an affectation as when the preacher wrote in the margin of his sermon, 'Cry here,' 'Smile here.' Why, if the man preached from his heart, he would be sure to cry in the right place and to smile at a suitable moment; and when the spiritual life is sound, it produces prayer at the right time, and humiliation of soul and sacred joy spring forth spontaneously, apart from rules and vows."[565]

Salary

What if the church fails to supply the minister's financial needs?

"When a minister is poorly remunerated and he feels that he is worth more and that the church could give him more, he ought kindly, boldly and firmly to communicate with the deacons first, and if they do not take it up, he should then mention it to the brethren in a sensible, business-like way, not as craving a charity, but as putting it to their sense of honor, that the 'laborer is worthy of his hire.'"[566]

(Spurgeon always upheld the maxim "The laborer is worthy his hire." To the officers of a small country church who sought him as their pastor but offered a ridiculously small salary he wrote:) "The only individual I know who could live on such a stipend…is the angel Gabriel. He would need neither cash nor clothes; and he could come down from Heaven every Sunday morning and go back at night, so I advise you to invite him."[567] "It is a remarkable fact that ministers of the Gospel are not able to live on much less than other people. They cannot make a schilling go far as other people can make a sovereign. Some of them try very hard but do not succeed. A member once said to a minister who wanted a little more salary as his family increased, 'I didn't know that you preached for money.'

"'No, I don't,' said the minister.

"'I thought you preached for souls.'

"'So, I do; but I could not live on souls, and if I could, it would take a good many the size of yours to make a meal.'"[568]

Selection, call of a pastor

Who possesses the sole authority in the selection of a minister to serve the church?

(Bill Brackney, professor of church history at Baylor University, answers, "He thought every church ought to have the right to select its own ministers, with no assistance from others in appointing him to the office."[569])

Self-examination

When is self-examination taken to the extreme?

"Self-examination is a very great blessing, but I have known self-examination carried on in a most unbelieving, legal, and self-righteous manner; in fact, I have so carried it on myself. Time was when I used to think a vast deal more of marks and signs and evidences for my own comfort than I do now, for I find that I cannot be a match for the Devil when I begin dealing in these things. I am obliged to go day by day with this cry: 'I the chief of sinners am, but Jesus died for me.' While I can believe the promise of God because it is His promise and because He is my God, and while I can trust my Savior because He is God and therefore mighty to save, all goes well with me; but I do find when I begin questioning myself about this and that perplexity, thus taking my eye off

Christ, that all the virtue of my life seems oozing out at every pore. Any practice that detracts from faith is an evil practice, but especially that kind of self-examination which would take us away from the cross-foot proceeds in a wrong direction."[570]

Sermon, borrowing from others

Is it proper to use another preacher's material (lumber)?

"He who will not use the thoughts of other men's brains proves he has no brains of his own."[571] (Several sermons Spurgeon preached were lifted directly from the works of Philip Doddridge and Richard Baxter and John Bunyan.[572] It indicates that he wasn't averse to using lumber from another's mill.)

Sermon, delivery

What constitutes good sermon delivery?

"Our preaching must not be articulate snoring. There must be power, life, energy, vigor. We must throw our whole selves into it and show that the zeal of God's house has eaten us up."[573]

"Let eloquence be flung to the dogs rather than souls be lost. What we want is to win souls. They are not won by flowery speeches."[574]

"If there be any brother here who thinks he can preach as well as he should, I would advise him to leave off altogether. There are brethren in the ministry whose speech is intolerable. I heard one say the other day that a certain preacher had no more gifts for the ministry than an oyster, and in my own judgment this was a slander on the oyster, for that worthy bivalve [a shell composed of two valves] shows great discretion in his openings and knows when to close. If some men were sentenced to hear their own sermons, it would be a righteous judgement upon them, and they would soon cry out with Cain, 'My punishment is greater than I can bear.'"[575]

Sermon, switching

Should I change sermons in the midst of a service?

(Spurgeon identifies with the struggle of changing messages in the midst of a service. One evening at New Park Street Chapel after he had announced the hymn preceding the sermon, he opened his Bible to the text that he had so well studied and prepared when a text on the opposite page jumped out at him as a lion from a thicket. Of that night he states,) "The people were singing and I was sighing. I was in a strait betwixt two, and my mind hung as in the balances. I was naturally desirous to run in the track which I had carefully planned, but the other text would take no refusal and seemed to tug at my skirts, crying, 'No, no, you must preach from me. God would have you follow me.' I deliberated within myself as to my duty, for I would neither be fanatical nor unbelieving, and at the last I thought within myself, *Well, I should like to preach the sermon which I have prepared, and it's a great risk to run to strike out a new line of thought, but still as this text constrains me, it may be of the Lord, and therefore I will venture upon it, come what may.*" (Spurgeon concluded,) "Anything is better than mechanical sermonizing in which the direction of the Spirit is practically ignored. Every Holy Ghost preacher, I have no doubt, will have such recollections clustering his ministry."[576] (Of that night he wrote,) "Some few church-meetings afterwards, two persons came forward to make confession of their faith, who professed to have been converted that evening."[577]

Sermon, text selection

How does the preacher know what to preach?

"Brethren, it is not easy for me to tell you precisely how I make my sermons. All through the week I am on the look-out for material that I can use on the Sabbath, but the actual work of arranging it is necessarily left until Saturday evening, for every other moment is fully occupied in the Lord's service. I have often said that my greatest difficulty is to fix my mind upon the particular texts which are to be the subjects of discourse on the following day, or, to speak more correctly, to know what topics the Holy Spirit would have me bring before the congregation. As soon as any passage of Scripture really grips my heart and soul, I concentrate my whole attention upon it, look at the precise meaning of the original, closely examine the context so as to see the special aspect of the text in its surroundings, and roughly jot down all the thoughts that occur to me concerning the subject, leaving to a later period the orderly marshaling of them for presentation to my hearers."[578]

> Wait for that elect word, even if you wait till within an hour of the service.
> Charles Spurgeon

"I confess that I frequently sit hour after hour praying and waiting for a subject, and that this is the main part of my study; much hard labor have I spent in manipulating topics, ruminating upon points of doctrine, making skeletons out of verses and then burying every bone of them in the catacombs of oblivion, sailing on and on over leagues of broken water till I see the red lights and make sail direct to the desired haven. I believe that almost any Saturday in my life I make enough outlines of sermons, if I felt at liberty to preach them, to last me for a month, but I no more dare to use them than an honest mariner would run to shore a cargo of contraband goods."[579]

"Wait for that elect word, even if you wait till within an hour of the service."[580] "Make your waiting upon God a necessity of your calling and at the same time the highest privilege of it. *Get your message fresh from God.* Even manna stinks if you keep it beyond its time; therefore, get it fresh from Heaven, and then it will have a celestial relish."[581]

"What a storehouse the Bible is since a man may continue to preach from it for years and still find that there is more to preach from than when he began to discourse upon it. There are hundreds of texts which remain like virgin summits, whereon the foot of the preacher has never trod. I might almost say that the major part of the Word of God is still in that condition: it is still an Eldorado unexplored, a land whose dust is gold. After thirty-five years I find the quarry of Holy Scripture is inexhaustible. I seem hardly to have begun to labor in it!"[582]

"Always make hay while the sun shines and store up notes of sermons when your mind is fertile, for there are seasons of famine as well as plenty, and every Joseph should lay up a store against the time of need."[583] (Thomas Spurgeon said of his father, "He had an overflowing store of information, and as he knew nothing of 'saving up' this or that for another occasion, each discourse was bright with fresh-cut flowers of speech and new-found gems of thought."[584])

Sermon, timespan

What is a good time frame for the sermon?

"In order to maintain attention, AVOID BEING TOO LONG. An old preacher used to say to a young man who preached an hour, 'My dear friend, I do not care what else you preach about, but I wish you would always preach about forty minutes.' We ought seldom to go much beyond that—forty minutes, or say three-quarters of an hour. If a fellow cannot say all he has to say in that time, when will he say it? But somebody said he liked 'to do justice to his subject.' Well, but ought he not to do justice to his people, or at least have a little mercy upon them and not keep them too long? The subject will not complain of you, but the people will....Brevity is a virtue within the reach of all of us; do not let us lose the opportunity of gaining the credit which it brings."[585]

"If you ask me how you may shorten your sermons, I should say *study them better.* Spend more time in the study that you may need less in the pulpit. We generally are longest when we have least to say."[586]

Sermon, prearranged

Should a preacher have pre-arranged sermons?

"I answer, every man in his own order. I am not a judge for others, but I dare not attempt such a thing and should signally fail if I were to venture upon it. Many eminent divines have delivered valuable courses of sermons on pre-arranged topics, but we are not eminent and must caution others like ourselves to be cautious how they act. Ordinarily, and for ordinary men, it seems to me that pre-arranged discourses are a mistake, are never more than an apparent benefit, and generally a real mischief. I dare not announce what I shall preach from tomorrow, much less what I shall preach from in six weeks or six months' time."[587]

Sermon, priority

What place should the minister give to the preparation of his sermon?

"Beware of running about from this meeting to that listening to mere twaddle and contributing your share to the general blowing up of windbags. A man great at tea drinkings, evening parties, and Sunday-school excursions is generally little everywhere else. Your pulpit preparations are your first business, and if you neglect these, you will bring no credit upon yourself or your office."[588]

Sin, its seriousness

How powerful and destructive is sin?

"Is it possible that one solitary sin could open the gates of Hell and then close them upon the guilty soul forever, and that God should refuse His mercy and shut out that soul forever from the presence of His face? Yes, if I believe my Bible, I must believe that. Oh, if we set our secret sins in the light of His mercy, if our transgressions are set side by side with His favors, we must each of us say our sins indeed are exceeding great!"[589]

Sorrow, bereavement (for widows of pastors)

A question for Mrs. Susannah Spurgeon, Spurgeon's wife, about coping with Charles's death.

What is your solace and consolation in the departure of Charles?

"In my deep and increasing loneliness, I still find sweetest comfort in praising God for His will concerning my beloved and myself and have even been able to thank Him for taking His dear servant from this sorrowful land of sin and darkness—to the bliss and glory of His eternal presence. Fixing my heart on the blessed fact that what the Lord does is right and best, simply because He does it, I feel the anchor hold in the depths of His love—and no tempest is powerful enough to drive faith's barque from these moorings. It can outride any storm with anchorage in such a haven. Many a time when the weight of my dreadful loss seemed as if it must crush me, it has been lifted by the remembrance that in Heaven my dear one is now perfectly praising his Lord, and that if I can sing too, I shall even here on earth be joining him in holy service and acceptable worship."[590]

Soulwinning

What value do you place on winning souls?

"I would rather be the means of saving [a soul] from death than to be the greatest orator on earth."[591] (Richard Day, in his biography of Spurgeon, states Spurgeon's "uncanny knowledge of the human heart and his wonderful skill in moving multitudes may be attributed largely to the hours he spent in the clinic of his personal intercourse with people [personal soulwinning]. [This, his hot passion for souls] is probably the precise explanation of his becoming one of the world's greatest preachers."[592])

How do you view pastors who fail to win souls?

"I am sure that if a minister wants conversions, he must identify himself with his people. There are people nowadays who make a difficulty about Moses praying for Israel, 'If thou wilt forgive their sin; and if not, blot me, I pray thee, out of thy book which thou hast written'; and they raise questions about Paul being willing to be separated from Christ for his brethren, his kinsmen according to the flesh. Oh, but there is no difficulty in the matter if you once get to feel such an intense love for the souls of men that you would, as it were, pawn your own salvation and count it little if you might but bring the people to the Savior's feet. A man who has never felt that willingness does not yet know the true throb of a pastor's heart."[593]

Is it easy for you to personally confront people about Christ?

"I often envy those of my brethren who can go up to individuals and talk to them with freedom about their souls. I do not always find myself able to do so; though, when I have been Divinely aided in such service, I have had a large reward."[594]

Soulwinning, church members

What role do church members play in the conversion of the lost at the Tabernacle?

"We owe very many of the conversions that have been wrought here to the personal exertions of our church members. God owns our ministry, but He also owns yours. It is to our delight at church-meetings that when converts come, they often have to say that the word preached from the pulpit was blessed to them, and yet I think that almost as often they say it was the word spoken in some of the classes, or in the pews, for not a few of you have been spiritual parents to strangers who have dropped in. Do this still. Let our congregation be full of these spiritual sharpshooters who shall pick out, each man his man, and who shall fire with the gun of the Gospel directly at each individual."[595]

How might the pastor induce his people to do soulwinning?

"In order to secure this end of gathering around you a band of Christians who will themselves be soul-winners, sometimes the very best plan would be to call all the members of the church together, tell them what you would like to see, and plead earnestly with them that each one should become for God a soul-winner. Say to them, 'I do not want to be your pastor simply that I may preach to you, but I long to see souls saved and to see those who are saved seeking to win others for the Lord Jesus Christ.' That might succeed in arousing them. Calling them together and earnestly pleading with them about the matter, pointing out what you wish them specially to do and to ask of God, may be like setting a light to dry fuel; but, on the other hand, nothing may come of it because of their lack of sympathy in the work of soul-saving. Your work, brethren, is to set your church on fire somehow. You may do it by speaking to the whole of the members, or you may do it by speaking to the few choice spirits, but you must do it somehow."[596]

Sovereignty of God

How do you reconcile the sovereignty of God and man's responsibility to repent?

"I do not try to reconcile friends—they are both in the Bible."[597]

Spiritual Development

What is the secret to spiritual progress?

"Work out your own salvation with fear and trembling. For it is God which worketh in you both to will and to do of his good pleasure" (Philippians 2:12b–13)[598]—(a favorite quote of Spurgeon.)

Study, the Scripture

What is your approach to hard-to-understand texts?

"When a text of Scripture lies, as it were, dead before us, we may not be able to understand it, but when by prayer the text grows into life and we set it in motion, we comprehend it at once. We may hammer away at a text sometimes in meditation and strike it again and again, and yet it may not yield to us, but we cry to God, and straightway the text opens, and we see concealed in it wondrous treasures of wisdom and of grace. But the prayer should not be merely that we may understand the text. I think we should pray over every passage in order that we may be enabled to get out of it what God would impart to us. A text is like a casket which is locked, and prayer is the key to open it, and then we get God's treasure. The text is God's letter, full of loving words, but prayer must break the seal."[599]

Success, pastoral

How is true success measured?

"The preacher may not get credit for his work in the statistics which reckon scores and hundreds, but in that other book which no secretary could keep, where things are weighed rather than numbered, the worker's register will greatly honor his Master."[600]

Suspiciousness, of church members

What do you say to the pastor who is suspicious of criticism toward him among church members?

"Do not, therefore, look about you with the eyes of mistrust, nor listen as an eavesdropper with the quick ear of fear. To go about the congregation ferreting out disaffection, like a gamekeeper after rabbits, is a mean employment and is generally rewarded most sorrowfully."[601] "It would be better to be deceived a hundred times than to live a life of suspicion. It is intolerable."[602] "Brethren, shun this vice by renouncing the love of self. Judge it to be a small matter what men think or say of you, and care only for their treatment of your Lord."[603]

Tracts, Gospel

A prominent preacher once said that tract distribution was "tacky evangelism." What saith you?

"I look upon the giving away of a religious tract as only the first step for action not to be compared with many another deed done for Christ, but were it not for the first step we might never reach to the second; but that first attained, we are encouraged to take another, and so at the last there is a real service of Christ in the distribution of the Gospel in its printed form, a service the result of which Heaven alone shall disclose and the judgment day alone discover. How many thousands have been carried to Heaven instrumentally upon the wings of these tracts, none can tell."[604]

"There is a way of giving a tract in the street which will ensure its kindly treatment, and another way which will prejudice the receiver against it; you can shove it into a person's hand so roughly that it is almost an insult, or you can hold it out so deftly that the passer-by accepts it with pleasure. Do not thrust it upon him as if it were a writ but invite him to accept it as if it were a ten-pound note."[605]

Visitation

Should soul-winning visitation be included in the pastor's schedule?

"Do not neglect visitation. It is true that I cannot visit my four thousand three hundred and fifty members. But my visitation is done by the elders. One young pastor lately said to me, 'I have no time to visit.'

'Goodness gracious!' said I, 'what have you got to do?'

'I have got my sermons to get up!'

'Yours sermons? Well, I suppose you are never in bed after six in the morning? From six to nine you have three hours—six times three is eighteen—that is, two clear days in the week of nine hours each. That ought to be enough time for your sermons—all before breakfast.' I do not say that everybody must get up so early in the morning, but I say we must make long days. Our days are so few that we make them long ones and take time by the forelock. Where there is a population of 500 in a town or village, no minister ought to rest satisfied until he has spoken to every accessible man about his soul."[606]

Worship, form

What comprised the worship service at the Tabernacle?

("Spurgeon believed that the elements of a church's worship gathering should only contain what God commands in Scripture [prayer, congregational singing, Scripture reading, preaching, and the ordinances of baptism and the Lord's Supper]."[607])

Should the service ever be varied?

"In order to prevent custom and routine from being enthroned among us, it will be well to *vary the order of service as much as possible*. Whatever the free Spirit moves us to do, that let us do at once....We hitherto understood that Baptist churches are not under bondage to traditions and fixed rules as to modes of worship, and yet these poor creatures, these would-be lords, who cry out loudly enough against a liturgy would bind their minister with rubrics made by custom. It is time that such nonsense were forever silenced. We claim to conduct service as the Holy Spirit moves us and as we judge best. We will not be bound to sing here and pray there but will vary the order of service to prevent monotony."[608]

Worship, at the Metropolitan Tabernacle

How did the worship service begin at the Tabernacle?

(Susannah Spurgeon and Joseph Harrald state in Spurgeon's autobiography, "Punctually at eleven o'clock, Mr. Spurgeon was seen descending the steps leading to the platform, followed by the long train of office-bearers [elders and deacons], and after a brief pause for silent supplication, the service began."[609])

How were services at the Tabernacle concluded?

"In pronouncing the solemn closing benediction [at the Tabernacle], we invoke on your behalf the love of Jesus Christ, the grace of the Father, and the fellowship of the Holy Spirit; and thus, according to the apostolic manner, we make a manifest distinction between the persons, showing that we believe the Father to be a person, the Son to be a person, and the Holy Ghost to be a person."[610]

Writing

What about writing books?

"It is a happy thing when the tongue is aided by the pen of a ready writer and so gets a wider sphere and a more permanent influence than if it merely uttered certain sounds and the words died away when the ear had heard them. The first thing which you have to do if God has called you to serve Him is after hearing what He has said to you, make it known to somebody else: 'Write the vision.' And take care, dear friends, that, in the spreading of truth, you *use as permanent a means of doing so as you can.* 'Write the vision'; that is to say, if you cannot write with the pen, if you have not that special gift, yet write it on men's hearts. Do not merely speak it but seek to reach the inmost soul of your fellow-beings, and by the power of the Holy Spirit write the truth there. God help you not merely to sound it in their ears, but to write it on the fleshy tablets of their heart and to leave the truth deeply engraved upon their memory!"[611]

"Let the Christian, whose hair is whitened by the sunlight of Heaven tell his life-long story."[612] (Spurgeon quoted Luther as saying,) "Luther once said, 'The devil hates goose quills,' and doubtless he has good reason, for ready writers, by the Holy Spirit's blessing, have done his kingdom much damage."[613]

Is it beneficial to keep a journal or diary?

"I have sometimes said when I have become the prey of doubting thoughts, *Well now, I dare not doubt whether there be a God, for I can look back in my Diary and say, 'On such a day, in the depths of trouble, I bent my knee to God, and or ever I had risen from my knees, the answer was given me.'*"[614]

Speaking at the Annual Conference of the Pastor's College in 1890

"I shall be gone from you ere long. You will meet and say to one another, 'The President has departed. What are we going to do?' I charge you, be faithful to the Gospel of our Lord Jesus Christ and the doctrine of His grace. Be ye faithful unto death, and your crowns will not be wanting. But, oh! let none of us die out dim candles. The Lord Himself bless you! Amen."[615]

~Charles Haddon Spurgeon

Appendix
Resources for the Preacher

Publications by Frank Shivers to assist the minister.

Evangelistic Preaching 101

The Evangelistic Invitation 101

Revivals 101

The Minister and the Funeral

Basics of Biblical Praying

How to Preach Without Evangelistic Results (Pamphlet & DVD)

Exposition of the Psalms (Three Volumes)

Life Principles from Proverbs

Spurs to Soul Winning

Evangelistic Praying

[1] Spurgeon, C. H. "Three Names High on the Muster-Roll." Sermon delivered August 16, 1891, Metropolitan Tabernacle.

[2] *The Life and Diary of David Brainerd,* 220.

[3] Spurgeon, C. H. "Christ's Loneliness and Ours." Sermon published August 8, 1907, Metropolitan Tabernacle.

[4] Spurgeon, C. H. *Autobiography,* Volume 2: *The Full Harvest 1860–1892.* (Carlisle, PA: The Banner of Truth Trust, 1973), v; and "Christ's Dying Word for His Church." Sermon delivered November 3, 1889, Metropolitan Tabernacle.

[5] Spurgeon, C. H. "Christ's Dying Word for His Church." Sermon delivered November 3, 1889, Metropolitan Tabernacle.

[6] Spurgeon, C. H. *Lectures to My Students: Addresses Delivered to the Students of the Pastor's College, Metropolitan Tabernacle. Second series.* (Vol. 2). (New York: Robert Carter and Brothers, 1889), 46.

[7] Spurgeon, C. H. *The Salt-cellars: Being a Collection of Proverbs, Together with Homely Notes Thereon.* (1889), 89.

[8] Spurgeon, C. H. *Autobiography,* Volume 2: *The Full Harvest 1860–1892.* (Carlisle, PA: The Banner of Truth Trust, 1973), 194.

[9] Spurgeon, C. H. *Faith's Checkbook,* Preface.

[10] Carlile, J.C. C. H. Spurgeon: An Interpretative Biography. (London: The Religious Tract Society and The Kingsgate Press, 1934), 305.

[11] Spurgeon, C. H. "Christ's Dying Word for His Church." Sermon delivered November 3, 1889, Metropolitan Tabernacle.

[12] Spurgeon, C. H. "Watching to See." Sermon delivered January 26, 1882, Metropolitan Tabernacle.

[13] Spurgeon, C. H. *An All-Round Ministry.* (Carlisle, PA: Banner of Truth Trust, 1978), 77.

[14] Harris, M. J. *The Second Epistle to the Corinthians: A Commentary on the Greek Text.* (Grand Rapids, MI; Milton Keynes, UK: W.B. Eerdmans Pub. Co.; Paternoster Press, 2005), 862.

[15] Spurgeon, C. H. "Not Sufficient, and Yet Sufficient." Sermon delivered August 24, 1890, Metropolitan Tabernacle.

[16] Spurgeon, C. H. *Faith's Checkbook,* December 16.

[17] Simeon, C. *Horae Homileticae: 2 Timothy to Hebrews,* (Vol. 19). (London: Holdsworth and Ball, 1833), 20.

[18] Spurgeon, C. H. "My Prayer." Sermon delivered September 22, 1872, Metropolitan Tabernacle.

[19] Spurgeon, C. H. "A Wafer of Honey." Sermon delivered in 1863, Metropolitan Tabernacle, published February 8, 1906.

[20] Morgan, Richard, Howard, and John. "G. Campbell Morgan: Preaching in the Shadow of Grace," https://www.preaching.com/articles/past-masters/g-campbell-morgan-preaching-in-the-shadow-of-grace/, accessed August 11, 2021.

[21] Spurgeon, C. H. "Feathers for Arrows: Or Illustrations for Preachers and Teachers, from My Note Book." (London: Passmore & Alabaster, 1870), 6.

[22] *The Christian Treasury,* (Contributions from Ministers and Members). (London: Groombridge and Son, 1868).

[23] Smith, James. "Be Strong in Grace" (1860). https://www.gracegems.org/Smith1/be_strong_in_grace.htm, accessed October 29, 2022.

[24] Exell, J. S. *The Biblical Illustrator: Romans* (Vol. 1). (New York; Chicago; Toronto; London; Edinburgh: Fleming H. Revell Company, n.d.), 14.

[25] Spurgeon, C. H. *Lectures to My Students: Addresses Delivered to the Students of the Pastor's College, Metropolitan Tabernacle. Second series.* (Vol. 2). (New York: Robert Carter and Brothers, 1889), 14.

[26] Spurgeon, C. H. "Preach the Gospel." Sermon delivered August 5, 1855, New Park Street Chapel.

[27] Newton, John. *The Works of John Newton.* (Vol. 5), 62.

[28] Lloyd-Jones, D. Martyn. *Preaching and Preachers.* (Grand Rapids: Zondervan, 2011), 130.

[29] Spurgeon, C. H. *Lectures to My Students: Addresses Delivered to the Students of the Pastor's College, Metropolitan Tabernacle. Second series.* (Vol. 2). (New York: Robert Carter and Brothers, 1889), 22–23.

[30] Spurgeon, C. H. "The Minister's Trumpet Blast and Church Member's Warning." Sermon delivered January 8, 1860, New Park Street Chapel.

[31] https://www.azquotes.com/quote/1403547, accessed October 30, 2022.

[32] Spence-Jones, H. D. M. (Ed.). *1 Corinthians.* (London; New York: Funk & Wagnalls Company, 1909), 300.

[33] Spurgeon, C. H. "Preach the Gospel." Sermon delivered August 5, 1855, New Park Street Chapel.

[34] Spurgeon, C. H. *2,200 Quotations: From the Writings of Charles H. Spurgeon: Arranged Topically or Textually and Indexed by Subject, Scripture, and People,* (T. Carter, Ed.). (Grand Rapids, MI: Baker Books, 1995), 161.

[35] Beeke, Joel. professor at Puritan Reformed Theological Seminary. https://www.azquotes.com/quote/911798, accessed October 11, 2022.

[36] Erwin Lutzer. "Still Called to the Ministry," *Moody Monthly* 83, no. 7, March 1983, 133.

[37] Bridges, Charles. *Christian Ministry*. 1830.

[38] Spurgeon, C. H. *Only a Prayer Meeting*. (Great Britain: Christian Focus Publications, 2000), 81.

[39] Spurgeon, C. H. *The Sword and the Trowel*. (London: Passmore & Alabaster, 1887), 122.

[40] Spurgeon, C. H. *An All-Round Ministry*. (Carlisle, PA: Banner of Truth Trust, 1978), 280.

[41] Exell, J. S. *The Biblical Illustrator: Galatians*. (New York; Chicago; Toronto; London; Edinburgh: Fleming H. Revell Company, n.d.), 512.

[42] Spurgeon, C. H. "The Secret Power in Prayer." Sermon delivered January 8, 1888, Metropolitan Tabernacle.

[43] Williams, W. *Personal Reminiscences of Charles Haddon Spurgeon*. (London: The Gospel Tract Society, 1895), 32.

[44] Spurgeon, C. H. "Pray Without Ceasing." Sermon delivered March 10, 1872. Metropolitan Tabernacle Pulpit, Volume 18.

[45] Spurgeon, C. H. "Unseasonable Prayer." Sermon delivered October 14, 1877, Metropolitan Tabernacle.

[46] Spurgeon, C. H. *The Complete Works of C. H. Spurgeon, Volume 14: Sermons 788 to 847*. (Delmarva Publications, Inc., 2015), 313.

[47] Tozer, A. W. *God Tells the Man Who Cares*, 3.

[48] Pierson, A. T. *From the Pulpit to the Palm-Branch: A Memorial of C. H. Spurgeon*. (London: Alabaster, Passmore and Sons, 1902), 11.

[49] Adcock, E. F. *Charles H. Spurgeon: Prince of Preachers*. (Anderson, Indiana: Gospel Tract Company, 1925), 94–95.

[50] Ibid.

[51] Cited in I. D. E. Thomas. *A Puritan Golden Treasury*. (Edinburgh: Banner of Truth, 1977), 192.

[52] Spurgeon, C. H. *Lectures to My Students: Addresses Delivered to the Students of the Pastor's College, Metropolitan Tabernacle. Second series*. (Vol. 2). (New York: Robert Carter and Brothers, 1889), 231.

[53] Ibid., 43.

[54] Ibid., 42.

[55] Ibid., 233.

[56] Spurgeon, C. H. "The Secret of Power in Prayer." Sermon delivered January 8, 1888, Metropolitan Tabernacle.

[57] Spurgeon, C. H. "Do You Know Him?" Sermon delivered January 31, 1864, Metropolitan Tabernacle.

[58] Spurgeon, C. H. Peace by Believing. Sermon delivered in 1863, Metropolitan Tabernacle.

[59] Cook, Charles. *Behold the Throne of Grace: Charles Spurgeon's Prayers,* Foreword.

[60] Spurgeon, C. H. "The Statute of David for the Sharing of the Spoil." Sermon delivered June 7, 1891, Metropolitan Tabernacle (one of the last sermons Spurgeon preached).

[61] Spurgeon, C. H. *Autobiography,* Volume 2: *The Full Harvest 1860–1892.* (Carlisle, PA: The Banner of Truth Trust, 1973).

[62] Spurgeon, C. H. "One Worker Preparing for Another." Sermon delivered August 14, 1890, Metropolitan Tabernacle.

[63] Spurgeon, Susannah and William Harrald. Autobiography of Charles H. Spurgeon Compiled from His Diary, Letters, and Records (Vol. 2). (1898), 354.

[64] Spurgeon, C. H. *Lectures to My Students: Addresses Delivered to the Students of the Pastor's College, Metropolitan Tabernacle. Second series.* (Vol. 2). (New York: Robert Carter and Brothers, 1889), 15.

[65] Young, Dinsdale. *Spurgeon's Pulpit Prayers.* (Passmore & Alabaster, 1905), Introduction.

[66] Dixon, A. C. *Evangelistic Work,* 166.

[67] MacArthur, J., Jr. (Ed.). *The MacArthur Study Bible* (electronic ed.). (Nashville, TN: Word Pub., 1997), 1771.

[68] Autrey, C. E. Basic Evangelism. (Grand Rapids: Zondervan, 1968), 33.

[69] Spurgeon, C. H. "Under Constraint." Sermon delivered April 28, 1878, Metropolitan Tabernacle.

[70] Exell, J. S. *The Biblical Illustrator: Second Corinthians*. (New York; Chicago; Toronto; London; Edinburgh: Fleming H. Revell Company, n.d.), 272. Alexander Maclaren. "Consuming Love" (Sermon).

[71] https://www.crosswalk.com/faith/spiritual-life/inspiring-quotes/21-challenging-quotes-about-gods-love.html, accessed November 3, 2022.

[72] Maclaren, Alexander. "Debtor to All Men," Romans 1:14.

[73] Spurgeon, C. H. "The Christian—a Debtor." Sermon delivered August 10, 1856.

[74] Spurgeon, C. H. "Under Constraint." Sermon delivered April 28, 1878, Metropolitan Tabernacle.

[75] Ibid.

[76] Spurgeon, C. H. "The Security of Believers; or, Sheep Who Shall Never Perish." Sermon delivered September 5, 1889, Metropolitan Tabernacle.

[77] Pink, A. W. *Gleanings from Paul on Prayer*, 18. "Prayer for Comprehension of God's Love."

[78] Spurgeon, C. H. "A Woman's Memorial." Sermon delivered November 28, 1859, New Park Street Chapel.

[79] Edwards, John. Veritas Redux, (Volume 3). (T. Cox, at The Lamb, under the Royal Exchange, 1726), 383.

[80] Spurgeon, C. H. "Paul the Ready." Sermon delivered May 22, 1890, Metropolitan Tabernacle.

[81] Ibid.

[82] Ibid.

[83] Ibid.

[84] Ibid.

[85] Raleigh, A. "Faithful unto Death." *The Biblical Illustrator,* Revelation 2:10.

[86] Spurgeon, C. H. "The Scales of Judgment." Sermon delivered June 12, 1859, New Park Street Chapel.

[87] MacArthur, J., Jr. (Ed.). *The MacArthur Study Bible* (electronic ed.). (Nashville, TN: Word Pub., 1997), 1743.

[88] Lowery, D. K. In J. F. Walvoord, R. B. Zuck (Eds.), *The Bible Knowledge Commentary: An Exposition of the Scriptures,* (Vol. 2). (Wheaton, IL: Victor Books, 1985), 1 Corinthians, 525.

[89] https://www.preceptaustin.org/1_corinthians_927_commentary, accessed November 4, 2022.

[90] Henry, M. *Matthew Henry's Commentary on the Whole Bible: Complete and Unabridged in One Volume.* (Peabody: Hendrickson, 1994), 2261.

[91] Ibid. Adapted. He used the word "apostasy"; I altered it to the word "castaway."

[92] Exell, J. S. *The Biblical Illustrator: First Corinthians*. (New York; Chicago; Toronto; London; Edinburgh: Fleming H. Revell Company, n.d.), 274.

[93] Spurgeon, C. H. "The Heavenly Race." Sermon delivered June 11, 1858, New Park Street Chapel.

[94] Spurgeon, C. H. *An All-Round Ministry.* (Carlisle, PA: Banner of Truth Trust, 1978), 76–77.

[95] Spurgeon, C. H. "The King's Weighings." Sermon delivered August 26, 1883, Metropolitan Tabernacle.

[96] Spurgeon, C. H. *Spurgeon's Bible Commentary,* 1 Corinthians 9:27.

[97] *A Memoir of the Life and Labors of the Rev. Adoniram Judson,* 33–34.

[98] Henry, M. *Matthew Henry's Commentary on the Whole Bible: Complete and Unabridged in One Volume.* (Peabody: Hendrickson, 1994), 2407.

[99] Spurgeon, C. H. "The Rule of the Race." Sermon delivered August 5, 1888, Metropolitan Tabernacle.

[100] Edwards, John. Veritas Redux, (Volume 3). (T. Cox, at The Lamb, under the Royal Exchange, 1726), 383.

[101] Spurgeon, C. H. *Autobiography, Vol. 1: The Early Years 1834-1859.* (London: Passmore & Alabaster, 1897), 175.

[102] "The Love of Charles and Susannah Spurgeon." https://www.christianity.com/church/church-history/timeline/2001-now/the-love-of-charles-and-susannah-spurgeon-11633045.html, accessed November 2, 2022.

[103] Charles Spurgeon Collection: Spurgeon, C. H. *John Ploughman's Talk:* Chapter 17: "A Good Word for Wives."

[104] Allen, James T. *Life Story of C. H. Spurgeon,* Chapter 7.

[105] Spurgeon, C. H. *Autobiography,* Volume 2: *The Full Harvest 1860–1892.* (Carlisle, PA: The Banner of Truth Trust, 1973), 180.

[106] Ibid.

[107] *Saturday Review:* "Politics, Literature, Science and Art," Volume 20. (London: Published at the Office, SouthHampton Street, Strand, 1865), 517.

[108] Spurgeon, C. H. *Autobiography,* Volume 2: *The Full Harvest 1860–1892.* (Carlisle, PA: The Banner of Truth Trust, 1973), 180.

[109] Ibid., 294.

[110] Ibid., 295.

[111] Ray, Charles. Charles Haddon Spurgeon. (London: Passmore & Alabaster, 1903), 414.

[112] https://www.reformedreader.org/rbb/spurgeon/conwell/bosch11.htm, accessed January 7, 2023.

[113] Spurgeon, C. H. *Come Ye Children.* (London: Passmore and Alabaster 1897), Chapter 22.

[114] Spurgeon, C. H. *Autobiography,* Volume 2: *The Full Harvest 1860–1892.* (Carlisle, PA: The Banner of Truth Trust, 1973), 270.

[115] Hayden, Eric W. "Charles H. Spurgeon: Did You Know?," https://www.christianitytoday.com/history/issues/issue-29/charles-h-spurgeon-did-you-know.html, accessed November 19, 2022.

[116] Spurgeon, C. H. *Autobiography,* Volume 2: *The Full Harvest 1860–1892.* (Carlisle, PA: The Banner of Truth Trust, 1973), 278–279.

[117] Ulmer, Selah. "3 Things You Didn't Know About Spurgeon's Wife," October 17, 2017. https://www.spurgeon.org/resource-library/blog-entries/3-things-you-didnt-know-about-spurgeons-wife/, accessed November 19, 2022.

[118] Rhodes, Ray, Jr. "Who Was Susannah Spurgeon?—5 Important Things You Need to Know." August 12, 2022. https://www.christianity.com/wiki/people/who-was-susannah-spurgeon.html, accessed November 1, 2022.

[119] Spurgeon, C. H. *Autobiography, Vol. 1: The Early Years 1834-1859.* (London: Passmore & Alabaster, 1897), 24.

[120] Chapter 11, "Lovely Westwood." https://www.reformedreader.org/rbb/spurgeon/conwell/bosch11.htm, accessed January 7, 2023.

[121] "The Love of Charles and Susannah Spurgeon." https://www.christianity.com/church/church-history/timeline/2001now/the-love-of-charles-and-susannah-spurgeon-11633045.html, accessed January 7, 2022.

[122] Bromehead, Joseph. "Jerusalem, My Glorious Home," 1886.

[123] Spurgeon, C. H. *Morning and Evening.* (Great Britain: Christian Focus Publications, 1994), March 20 (Evening).

[124] Spurgeon, C. H. *Lectures to My Students: Addresses Delivered to the Students of the Pastor's College, Metropolitan Tabernacle. Second series.* (Vol. 2). (New York: Robert Carter and Brothers, 1889), 197.

[125] Spurgeon, C. H. "The King and His Court." Sermon delivered March 11, 1888, Metropolitan Tabernacle.

[126] Spurgeon, C. H. The Infallibility of Scripture. Sermon delivered March 11, 1888, Metropolitan Tabernacle.

[127] Spurgeon, C. H. *Lectures to My Students: Addresses Delivered to the Students of the Pastor's College, Metropolitan Tabernacle. Second series.* (Vol. 2). (New York: Robert Carter and Brothers, 1889), 17–18.

[128] Ibid., 185–186.

[129] Spurgeon, C. H. *Lectures to My Students: Addresses Delivered to the Students of the Pastor's College, Metropolitan Tabernacle. Second series.* (Vol. 2). (New York: Robert Carter and Brothers, 1889), 32.

[130] Spurgeon, C. H. "Preach the Gospel." Sermon delivered August 5, 1855, New Park Street Chapel.

[131] Spurgeon, C. H. "A Revival Promise." Sermon delivered January 11, 1874, Metropolitan Tabernacle.

[132] Spurgeon, C. H. "Election: Its Defences and Evidences." Sermon delivered February 2, 1862, Metropolitan Tabernacle.

[133] Murray, Ian. *The Forgotten Spurgeon.* (Edinburgh: The Banner of Truth Trust, 1986), 38.

[134] Hayden, Eric W. "The Spurgeon Archive." https://archive.spurgeon.org/spurgn2.php, accessed October 24, 2022.

[135] "3 Ways the Holy Spirit Helped Spurgeon Preach." https://www.spurgeon.org/resource-library/blog-entries/3-ways-the-holy-spirit-helped-spurgeon-preach/, accessed December 13 2022.

[136] Spurgeon, C. H. *An All-Round Ministry.* (Carlisle, PA: Banner of Truth Trust, 1978), 320–321.

[137] Ibid., 328.

[138] Ray, Charles. *A Marvellous Ministry.* (London: Passmore & Alabaster, 1905), Chapter Four, "A Remarkable Growth."

[139] Spurgeon, C. H. "My Prayer." Sermon delivered September 22, 1872, Metropolitan Tabernacle.

[140] Spurgeon, C. H. "The Wedding Was Furnished with Guests." Sermon delivered May 6, 1888, Metropolitan Tabernacle.

[141] Spurgeon, C. H. "Our Urgent Need of the Holy Spirit." Sermon delivered January 7, 1877, Metropolitan Tabernacle.

[142] Spurgeon, C. H. "The Holy Spirit's Chief Office." Sermon delivered July 26, 1888, Metropolitan Tabernacle.

[143] Spurgeon, C. H. *Lectures to My Students: Addresses Delivered to the Students of the Pastor's College, Metropolitan Tabernacle. Second series.* (Vol. 2). (New York: Robert Carter and Brothers, 1889), 315.

[144] Spurgeon, C. H. "He Blessed Him There." Sermon delivered, Metropolitan Tabernacle. A sermon published on Thursday, October 13, 1910.

[145] Spurgeon, C. H. *Lectures to My Students: Addresses Delivered to the Students of the Pastor's College, Metropolitan Tabernacle.* (Vol. 1). (London: Passmore and Alabaster, 1875), 2.

[146] Exell, J. S. *The Biblical Illustrator: Leviticus and Numbers* (Vol. 1). (New York; Chicago; Toronto; London; Edinburgh: Fleming H. Revell Company, n.d.), 107.

[147] Symington, Andrew James. *Thomas Guthrie: A Biographical Sketch.* (London: Houlston & Sons, 1879), 153.

[148] Exell, J. S. *The Biblical Illustrator: Leviticus and Numbers* (Vol. 1). (New York; Chicago; Toronto; London; Edinburgh: Fleming H. Revell Company, n.d.), 106.

[149] Spurgeon, C. H. *Morning and Evening.* (Great Britain: Christian Focus Publications, 1994), July 16 (Morning).

[150] Spurgeon, C. H. "God-Guided Men." Sermon delivered March 15, 1874, Metropolitan Tabernacle.

[151] Ibid.

[152] MacArthur, John. *Slave.* (Nashville: Thomas Nelson, 2010), 125.

[153] Bruce, F. F. *The Epistle to the Galatians: A Commentary on the Greek Text.* (Grand Rapids, MI: W.B. Eerdmans Pub. Co., 1982), 84.

[154] Spurgeon, C. H. "Behold the Lamb of God." Sermon delivered October 16, 1887, Metropolitan Tabernacle.

[155] https://www.christianquotes.info/top-quotes/15-impactful-quotes-about-approval-and-fitting-in/, accessed October 7, 2022.

[156] Spurgeon, C. H. "Forty Years." Sermon delivered June 14 1874, Metropolitan Tabernacle.

[157] Spurgeon quoted the poem in the sermon "Forty Years" without citing an author. We do know that Richard Baxter's poem is the source for the last two lines [*Baxter's Poetical Fragments* (1st ed.), (1681), 40, lines 7–8.]

[158] Stott, John. "Langham Partnership Daily Thought, a Service of Langham Partnership International and John Stott Ministries." October 23, 2011.

[159] Exell, J. S. *The Biblical Illustrator: Galatians.* (New York; Chicago; Toronto; London; Edinburgh: Fleming H. Revell Company, n.d.), 33.

[160] Spurgeon, C. H. *Lectures to My Students: Addresses Delivered to the Students of the Pastor's College, Metropolitan Tabernacle. Second series.* (Vol. 2). (New York: Robert Carter and Brothers, 1889), 158.

[161] https://www.biblia.work/sermons/burdened/, accessed December 12, 2022.

[162] *Expositor's Greek Testament,* Mark 6:31.

[163] Spurgeon, C. H. *Lectures to My Students: Addresses Delivered to the Students of the Pastor's College, Metropolitan Tabernacle. Second series.* (Vol. 2). (New York: Robert Carter and Brothers, 1889), 158.

[164] https://www.allchristianquotes.org/quotes/Mike_Yaconelli/6988/, accessed November 22, 2022.

[165] MacArthur, J., Jr. (Ed.). *The MacArthur Study Bible* (electronic ed.). (Nashville, TN: Word Pub., 1997), 1668 (Acts 18:22–23).

[166] Spurgeon, C. H. *Lectures to My Students: Addresses Delivered to the Students of the Pastor's College, Metropolitan Tabernacle. Second series.* (Vol. 2). (New York: Robert Carter and Brothers, 1889), 160 -161.

[167] Ibid., 158.

[168] Ibid.

[169] Hayden, Eric W. (former Pastor at Metropolitan Tabernacle). Cited in the *Christian History Magazine,* Issue 29, 2–3. Copyright © 1991 by Christian History.

[170] Spurgeon, C. H. *Autobiography,* Volume 2: *The Full Harvest 1860–1892.* (Carlisle, PA: The Banner of Truth Trust, 1973), 18.

[171] Spurgeon, C. H. "For the Sick and Afflicted." Sermon delivered January 22, 1876, Metropolitan Tabernacle.

[172] Dallimore, Arnold. *A New Biography.* (Pennsylvania, Banner of Trust, 2005).

[173] Drummond, Lewis A. *Spurgeon: Prince of Preachers.* (Grand Rapids: Kregel Publications, 1992), 456.

[174] Spurgeon, in a letter from Mentone, written in 1882 and cited in Spurgeon, C. H. *Autobiography,* Volume 2: *The Full Harvest 1860–1892.* (Carlisle, PA: The Banner of Truth Trust, 1973), 368.

[175] Spurgeon, C. H. "Harvest Joy." Sermon delivered July 6, 1890, Metropolitan Tabernacle.

[176] Hayden, Eric. *Highlights in the Life of C. H. Spurgeon.* (Pilgrim Publications, 1990), 103. Cited in John Piper, "Charles Spurgeon: Preaching through Adversity." (Sermon, January 31, 1995, 1995 Bethlehem Conference of Pastors).

[177] "22 Spurgeon Quotes for Surviving Life's Storms," October 25, 2016 (Staff). https://www.spurgeon.org/resource-library/blog-entries/22-spurgeon-quotes-for-surviving-lifes-storms/, accessed December 5, 2022.

[178] Allen, James T. *Life Story of C. H. Spurgeon,* Chapter 7.

[179] Exell, J. S. *The Biblical Illustrator: St. Mark.* (New York; Chicago; Toronto; London; Edinburgh: Fleming H. Revell Company, n.d.), 251.

[180] Ibid, 249.

[181] A facsimile of the letter is found in Spurgeon, C. H. *Autobiography,* Volume 2: *The Full Harvest 1860–1892.* (Carlisle, PA: The Banner of Truth Trust, 1973), 15–16 (Illustrations).

[182] Spurgeon, C. H. *Lectures to My Students: Addresses Delivered to the Students of the Pastor's College, Metropolitan Tabernacle. Second series.* (Vol. 2). (New York: Robert Carter and Brothers, 1889), 214.

[183] Spurgeon, C. H. "The Rule of the Race." Sermon delivered August 5, 1888, Metropolitan Tabernacle.

[184] *Barnes Notes on the Bible*, Psalm 20:7.

[185] Plumer, W. S. Studies in the Book of Psalms: Being a Critical and Expository Commentary, with Doctrinal and Practical Remarks on the Entire Psalter. (Philadelphia; Edinburgh: J. B. Lippincott Company; A & C Black, 1872), 273.

[186] Chambers, Oswald. *My Utmost for His Highest,* April 23 entry.

[187] https://latefaith.com/quotes-about-focusing-on-god, accessed December 12, 2022.

[188] Spurgeon, C. H. *Lectures to My Students: Addresses Delivered to the Students of the Pastor's College, Metropolitan Tabernacle. Second series.* (Vol. 2). (New York: Robert Carter and Brothers, 1889), 214.

[189] Exell, J. S. *The Biblical Illustrator: Leviticus and Numbers* (Vol. 1). (New York; Chicago; Toronto; London; Edinburgh: Fleming H. Revell Company, n.d.), 110.

[190] Spurgeon, C. H. "The Best Christmas Fare." Sermon delivered December 25, 1881, Metropolitan Tabernacle.

[191] *Barnes Notes on the Bible*, Ephesians 6:17.

[192] Clarke, Adam. *Commentary on the Bible.* (1831), Ephesians 6:17.

[193] Exell, J. S. *The Biblical Illustrator: Ephesians.* (New York; Chicago; Toronto; London; Edinburgh: Fleming H. Revell Company, n.d.), 674.

[194] Spurgeon, C. H. "The Word of a King." Sermon delivered March 22, 1873, Metropolitan Tabernacle.

[195] Spurgeon, C. H. "A Description of Young Men in Christ." Sermon delivered April 8, 1883.

[196] Ibid.

[197] Spurgeon, C. H. *The Greatest Fight in the World.* (Gideon House Books, 2016), 10.

[198] Spurgeon, C. H. "The Word of a King." Sermon delivered March 22, 1873, Metropolitan Tabernacle.

[199] Spurgeon, C. H. *Lectures to My Students: Addresses Delivered to the Students of the Pastor's College, Metropolitan Tabernacle.* (Vol. 1). (London: Passmore and Alabaster, 1875), 195.

[200] Spurgeon, C. H. "The Last Words of Christ on the Cross." Sermon delivered June 25, 1882, Metropolitan Tabernacle.

[201] Spurgeon, C. H. *Morning and Evening.* (Great Britain: Christian Focus Publications, 1994), October 12 (Morning).

[202] Spurgeon, C. H. "The Sword of the Spirit." Sermon delivered April 19, 1891, Metropolitan Tabernacle.

[203] Spurgeon, C. H. "The Folly of Unbelief." Sermon delivered August 28, 1887, Metropolitan Tabernacle.

[204] Spurgeon, C. H. "The Sword of the Spirit." Sermon delivered April 19, 1891, Metropolitan Tabernacle.

[205] Henry, Matthew. *Matthew Henry's Concise Commentary,* 1 Samuel 17:39.

[206] Spurgeon, C. H. *An All-Round Ministry.* (Carlisle, PA: Banner of Truth Trust, 1978), 73–74.

[207] Spurgeon, C. H. *Morning and Evening.* (Great Britain: Christian Focus Publications, 1994), July 18 (Evening).

[208] McGee, J. V. *Thru the Bible Commentary: History of Israel (1 and 2 Samuel)* (electronic ed., Vol. 12). (Nashville: Thomas Nelson, 1991), 99.

[209] Spurgeon, C. H. *An All-Round Ministry.* (Carlisle, PA: Banner of Truth Trust, 1978), 233.

[210] Charles Spurgeon Collection: Spurgeon, C. H. *John Ploughman's Talk:* Chapter 22: "Try."

[211] Maclaren, Alexander. "God's Fighters Not to Take the Weapons of the World." *The Biblical Illustrator,* 1 Samuel 17:39.

[212] Maclaren, Alexander. "Commentary on Hebrews 4." Alexander Maclaren's Expositions of Holy Scripture. https://www.studylight.org/commentaries/eng/mac/hebrews-4.html, accessed June 18, 2021.

[213] Stewart, James. *Heralds of God.* (Grand Rapids: Baker Book House, 1972),186–187.

[214] Exell, J. S. *The Biblical Illustrator: Ephesians.* (New York; Chicago; Toronto; London; Edinburgh: Fleming H. Revell Company, n.d.), 371.

[215] Spence-Jones, H. D. M. (Ed.). *Ephesians.* (London; New York: Funk & Wagnalls Company, 1909), 148.

[216] "A Plea for Clarity in Preaching," http://www.preaching.com/resources/articles/11563696, accessed November 24, 2013.

[217] Courson, J. *Jon Courson's Application Commentary.* (Nashville, TN: Thomas Nelson, 2003), 1250.

[218] Spurgeon, C. H. "Freshness." Sermon delivered February 16, 1882, Metropolitan Tabernacle.

219 Spurgeon, C. H. "How to Read the Bible." Sermon delivered June 21, 1866, Metropolitan Tabernacle.

220 Spurgeon, C. H. "Paul the Ready." Sermon delivered May 22, 1890, Metropolitan Tabernacle.

221 Chambers, Oswald. *My Utmost for His Highest,* November 25 entry.

222 Spurgeon, C. H. "The Best Bread." Sermon delivered October 28, 1886, Metropolitan Tabernacle.

223 Spurgeon, C. H. "Grand Glorying." Sermon delivered July 5, 1868, Metropolitan Tabernacle.

224 Spurgeon, C. H. *The Soulwinne.* (New Kensington, PA: Whitaker House, 1995), 253.

225 Spurgeon, C. H. "To You." Sermon delivered July 9, 1876, Metropolitan Tabernacle.

226 "6 Quotes Spurgeon Didn't Say," August 8, 2017. https://www.spurgeon.org/resource-library/blog-entries/6-quotes-spurgeon-didnt-say/, accessed October 25, 2022. The quote "I take my text and make a beeline to the Cross," though credited to Spurgeon, is not found in any of his sermons or books. However, in main it exhibits his manner of preaching.

227 Spurgeon, C. H. "Christ Precious to Believers." Sermon delivered March 30, 1890, Metropolitan Tabernacle.

228 Spurgeon, C. H. *Lectures to My Students: Addresses Delivered to the Students of the Pastor's College, Metropolitan Tabernacle. Second series.* (Vol. 2). (New York: Robert Carter and Brothers, 1889), 75–76.

229 Quayle, William A. *The Pastor-Preacher.* (New York: The Methodist Book Concern, 1910), 55.

230 Exell, J. S. *The Biblical Illustrator: First Corinthians.* (New York; Chicago; Toronto; London; Edinburgh: Fleming H. Revell Company, n.d.), 119.

231 Spurgeon, C. H. "Preach the Gospel." Sermon delivered August 5, 1855, New Park Street Chapel.

232 Spurgeon, C. H. *2,200 Quotations: From the Writings of Charles H. Spurgeon: Arranged Topically or Textually and Indexed by Subject, Scripture, and People,* (T. Carter, Ed.). (Grand Rapids, MI: Baker Books, 1995), 157.

233 Spurgeon, C. H. *Sermons in Candles,* Lecture One.

234 Roloff, Lester. *The Family Altar.* (Number 4), 8.

235 Spurgeon, C. H. *An All-Round Ministry.* (Carlisle, PA: Banner of Truth Trust, 1978), 165.

[236] This material was adapted from the work of Jerry Harmon in the *Journal of the Grace Evangelical Society*, Spring, 2006.

[237] Hayden, Eric. *Searchlight on Spurgeon.* (Pasadena, TX: Pilgrim Publications, 1973), 7.

[238] Drummond, Lewis A. *Spurgeon: Prince of Preachers.* (Grand Rapids: Kregel Publications, 1992), 658.

[239] Hayden, Eric. *Searchlight on Spurgeon.* (Pasadena, TX: Pilgrim Publications, 1973), 8.

[240] Spurgeon, C. H. *An All-Round Ministry.* (Carlisle, PA: Banner of Truth Trust, 1978), 236.

[241] Henry, M. *Matthew Henry's Commentary on the Whole Bible: Complete and Unabridged in One Volume.* (Peabody: Hendrickson, 1994), 2362.

[242] Criswell, W. A., P. Patterson, E. R. Clendenen, D. L. Akin, M. Chamberlin, D. K. Patterson & J. Pogue (Eds.). *Believer's Study Bible* (electronic ed.). (Nashville: Thomas Nelson, 1991), 1 Co 9:22.

[243] Spurgeon, C. H. "By All Means Save Some." Sermon delivered April 26, 1874, Metropolitan Tabernacle.

[244] Exell, J. S. *The Biblical Illustrator: First Corinthians* (Vol. 1). (New York; Chicago; Toronto; London; Edinburgh: Fleming H. Revell Company, n.d.), 546.

[245] Spurgeon, C. H. *Autobiography of Charles H. Spurgeon: Compiled from His Diary,* Volume 1. (Scotts Valley, CA: CreateSpace, 2017), 233.

[246] Spurgeon, C. H. "Preach the Gospel." Sermon delivered August 5, 1855, New Park Street Chapel.

[247] Spurgeon, C. H. *Lectures to My Students: Addresses Delivered to the Students of the Pastor's College, Metropolitan Tabernacle. Second series.* (Vol. 2). (New York: Robert Carter and Brothers, 1889), 240.

[248] Ibid.

[249] *The Spurgeon Study Bible*, 1 Corinthians 9:22.

[250] Spurgeon, C. H. *Lectures to My Students: Addresses Delivered to the Students of the Pastor's College, Metropolitan Tabernacle. Second series.* (Vol. 2). (New York: Robert Carter and Brothers, 1889), 66–67.

[251] Spurgeon, C. H. *The Sword and Trowel.* (February, 1866), "A Spur for a Free Horse."

[252] Spurgeon, C. H. *Lectures to My Students: Addresses Delivered to the Students of the Pastor's College, Metropolitan Tabernacle.* (Vol. 1). (London: Passmore and Alabaster, 1875), 189.

[253] Tozer, A. W. *The Works of A. W. Tozer.*

[254] Bounds, E. M. *Prayer and Praying Men*. (Scotts Valley, CA: CreateSpace, 2011), Chapter 14.

[255] Spurgeon, C. H. *Faith's Checkbook,* March 17 (Fear to Fear).

[256] Spurgeon, C. H. "Two Ancient Proverbs." Sermon delivered March 29, 1874, Metropolitan Tabernacle.

[257] Spurgeon, C. H. "Speak for Yourself. A Challenge!," Sermon delivered January 1, 1877, Metropolitan Tabernacle.

[258] Spurgeon, C. H. *Only a Prayer Meeting*. (Great Britain: Christian Focus Publications, 2000), 75.

[259] https://founders.org/2007/09/17/more-from-spurgeon-on-courage/, accessed October 27, 2022.

[260] Spurgeon, C. H. *Autobiography of Charles H. Spurgeon: 1834–1859.* (Chicago, NY and Toronto: Fleming Revell, 1899), 268.

[261] Spurgeon, C. H. *The Sword and the Trowel*. (London: Passmore & Alabaster, October 1887), 515.

[262] Ibid, 558.

[263] Ibid., (July 1888,) 343.

[264] Carlile, J.C. C. H. Spurgeon: An Interpretative Biography. (London: The Religious Tract Society and The Kingsgate Press, 1934), 244.
An Interpretative biography

[265] Spurgeon, C. H. *The Sword and the Trowel*. (London: Passmore & Alabaster, 1887), April.

[266] Spurgeon, C. H. *Faith's Checkbook,* March 17 (Fear to Fear).

[267] Spurgeon, C. H. "Three Names High on the Muster-Roll." Sermon delivered August 16, 1891, Metropolitan Tabernacle.

[268] Douglas, C. N. (comp.). *Forty Thousand Quotations: Prose and Poetical.* (New York: Halcyon House, 1917).

[269] www.whatchristianswanttoknow.com/bible-verses-about-worry-20-comforting-scripture-quotes, accessed September 4, 2017.

[270] Spurgeon, C. H. *Morning and Evening*. (Great Britain: Christian Focus Publications, 1994), December 28 (Evening).

[271] Ibid., May 11 (Evening).

[272] Spurgeon, C. H. "Man's Weakness and God's Strength," Lost Sermon No. 108.

[273] Spurgeon, C. H. "Indwelling Sin." Sermon delivered June 1, 1856, New Park Street Chapel.

[274] Spurgeon, C. H. "Hold Fast Your Shield." Sermon delivered October 27, 1861, Metropolitan Tabernacle.

[275] Spurgeon, C. H. "The Cause and Cure of a Wounded Spirit." Sermon delivered April 16, 1885, Metropolitan Tabernacle.

[276] Spurgeon, C. H. *The Sword and the Trowel.* (London: Passmore & Alabaster, 1892).

[277] https://www.princeofpreachers.org/quotes/category/promises-of-god, accessed November 9, 2022.

[278] Spurgeon, C. H. "A Vile Weed and a Fair Flower." Sermon delivered in 1878, Metropolitan Tabernacle.

[279] Spurgeon, C. H. "A Description of Young Men in Christ." Sermon delivered April 8, 1883. https://www.ccel.org/ccel/s/spurgeon/sermons29/cache/sermons29.pdf

[280] Spurgeon, C. H. *Faith's Checkbook,* Preface.

[281] Ibid.

[282] Exell, J. S. *The Biblical Illustrator: Second Corinthians.* (New York; Chicago; Toronto; London; Edinburgh: Fleming H. Revell Company, n.d.), 32.

[283] Spurgeon, C. H. *According to Promise: or the Method of the Lord's Dealings with His Chosen.* (New York: Funk & Wagnalls, 1887), 61.

[284] January 4, 2022—"Confidence in the Promises of God." https://www.crosswalk.com/devotionals/loveworthfinding/love-worth-finding-january-4-2022.html, accessed November 10, 2022.

[285] Spurgeon, C. H. "Not Bound Yet." Sermon delivered April 7, 1887, Metropolitan Tabernacle.

[286] Spurgeon, C. H. *Faith's Checkbook,* November 3.

[287] Spurgeon, C. H. "Living on the Word." Sermon delivered March 15, 1883, Metropolitan Tabernacle.

[288] Spurgeon, C. H. "The Hope Laid Up in Heaven." Sermon delivered October 13, 1878, Metropolitan Tabernacle.

[289] Wiersbe, W. W. *The Bible Exposition Commentary,* Vol. 1. (Wheaton, IL: Victor Books, 1996), 645.

[290] Exell, J. S. *The Biblical Illustrator: Second Corinthians.* (New York; Chicago; Toronto; London; Edinburgh: Fleming H. Revell Company, n.d.), 236.

[291] Spurgeon, C. H. *Morning and Evening.* (Great Britain: Christian Focus Publications, 1994), June 7 (Evening).

[292] Ibid., January 29 (Morning).

[293] Spurgeon, C. H. "The Hope Laid Up in Heaven." Sermon delivered October 13, 1878, Metropolitan Tabernacle.

[294] Spurgeon, C. H. "The Hope of Future Bliss." Sermon delivered May 20, 1855, Exeter Hall, Strand.

[295] Spurgeon, C. H. "The Anchor." Sermon delivered May 21, 1876, Metropolitan Tabernacle.

[296] Spurgeon, C. H. "Alto and Bass." Sermon delivered April 1, 1883, Metropolitan Tabernacle.

[297] Keller, Tim. "Quotes on Hope: 7 Memorable Statements From Christian Evangelist." *Newsmax,* Tuesday, 19 May 2015, accessed April 9, 2024.

[298] Piper, John. Devotional, January 20. "The Battle to Remind."

[299] Spurgeon quoted these lines in the sermon "The Sacred Love-Token," August 22, 1875.

[300] Spurgeon, C. H. "The Hope of Future Bliss." Sermon delivered May 20, 1855, Exeter Hall, Strand.

[301] Spurgeon, C. H. "Feeding on the Word." Sermon delivered May 8, 1890, Metropolitan Tabernacle.

[302] Henry, M. *Matthew Henry's Commentary on the Whole Bible: Complete and Unabridged in One Volume.* (Peabody: Hendrickson, 1994), 2262.

[303] Spurgeon, C. H. *Lectures to My Students: Addresses Delivered to the Students of the Pastor's College, Metropolitan Tabernacle. Second series.* (Vol. 2). (New York: Robert Carter and Brothers, 1889), 40–41.

[304] Henry, M. *Matthew Henry's Commentary on the Whole Bible: Complete and Unabridged in One Volume.* (Peabody: Hendrickson, 1994), 783.

[305] Spurgeon, C. H. The Treasury of David: Psalms 27–57 (Vol. 2). (London; Edinburgh; New York: Marshall Brothers, n.d.), 45.

[306] Spurgeon, C. H. "A Caution to the Presumptuous." Sermon delivered May 13 1855, New Park Street Chapel.

[307] Spurgeon, C. H. "Preach the Gospel." Sermon delivered August 5, 1855, New Park Street Chapel.

[308] Spurgeon, C. H. "A Special Benediction." Sermon delivered May 12, 1887, Metropolitan Tabernacle. See Expository Notes on Jude at its conclusion.

[309] Spurgeon, C. H. "Comfort for Tried Believers." Sermon delivered September 1, 1876, Metropolitan Tabernacle.

[310] *Expositor's Greek Testament,* 1 Corinthians 10:12.

[311] *Barnes Notes on the Bible*, 1 Corinthians 10:12.

[312] Henry, M. *Matthew Henry's Commentary on the Whole Bible: Complete and Unabridged in One Volume.* (Peabody: Hendrickson, 1994), 2262.

[313] Spurgeon, C. H. *Morning and Evening.* (Great Britain: Christian Focus Publications, 1994), January 17 (Evening).

[314] Spurgeon, C. H. "A Caution to the Presumptuous." Sermon delivered May 13 1855, New Park Street Chapel.

[315] Spurgeon, C. H. *Morning and Evening.* (Great Britain: Christian Focus Publications, 1994), March 14 (Morning).

[316] Spurgeon, C. H. "The Cause and Cure of Weariness in Sabbath-School Teachers." Sermon delivered November 8, 1887, Metropolitan Tabernacle.

[317] Spurgeon, C. H. "Christ's Loneliness and Ours." Sermon published August 8, 1907, Metropolitan Tabernacle.

[318] Spurgeon, C. H. The Treasury of David: Psalms 120–150 (Vol. 6). (London; Edinburgh; New York: Marshall Brothers, n.d.), 71.

[319] Exell, J. S. *The Biblical Illustrator: Isaiah* (Vol. 3) (New York; Chicago; Toronto; London; Edinburgh: Fleming H. Revell Company, n.d.), 258.

[320] Spurgeon, C. H. "Christ's Loneliness and Ours." Sermon published August 8, 1907, Metropolitan Tabernacle.

[321] Ibid.

[322] Ibid.

[323] Exell, J. S. *The Biblical Illustrator: Ecclesiastes & The Song of Solomon* (Vol. 1). (New York; Chicago; Toronto; London; Edinburgh: Fleming H. Revell Company, n.d.), 270.

[324] Melvill, H. "Spiritual Efforts Not Lost." https://biblehub.com/sermons/ecclesiastes/11-1.htm, accessed December 10, 2022.

[325] Spurgeon, C. H. *Lectures to My Students: Addresses Delivered to the Students of the Pastor's College, Metropolitan Tabernacle. Second series.* (Vol. 2). (New York: Robert Carter and Brothers, 1889), 174.

[326] Spurgeon, C. H. "The Cause and Cure of Weariness in Sabbath-School Teachers." Sermon delivered November 8, 1887, Metropolitan Tabernacle.

[327] Spurgeon, C. H. The Treasury of David: Psalms 120–150 (Vol. 6). (London; Edinburgh; New York: Marshall Brothers, n.d.), 70.

[328] Spurgeon, C. H. "Our Gifts, and How to Use Them." Sermon delivered in 1872, Metropolitan Tabernacle.

[329] MacArthur, J., Jr. (Ed.). *The MacArthur Study Bible* (electronic ed.). (Nashville, TN: Word Pub., 1997), 1875.

[330] Ibid.

[331] Wesley, J. *Wesley's Notes on the Bible,* 2 Timothy 1:6.

[332] Spurgeon, C. H. "Our Gifts, and How to Use Them." Sermon delivered in 1872, Metropolitan Tabernacle.

[333] Spurgeon, C. H. *Lectures to My Students: Addresses Delivered to the Students of the Pastor's College, Metropolitan Tabernacle. Second series.* (Vol. 2). (New York: Robert Carter and Brothers, 1889), 314.

[334] Spurgeon, C. H. "Our Gifts, and How to Use Them." Sermon delivered in 1872, Metropolitan Tabernacle.

[335] Ibid.

[336] Spurgeon, C. H. "Harvest Men Wanted." Sermon delivered August 17, 1873, Metropolitan Tabernacle.

[337] Spurgeon, C. H. "Prayer—the Forerunner of Mercy." Sermon delivered June 28, 1857, At the Music Hall, Surrey Gardens.

[338] Spurgeon, C. H. "Harvest Men Wanted." Sermon delivered August 17, 1873, Metropolitan Tabernacle.

[339] Spurgeon, C. H. *Lectures to My Students: Addresses Delivered to the Students of the Pastor's College, Metropolitan Tabernacle. Second series.* (Vol. 2). (New York: Robert Carter and Brothers, 1889), 93.

[340] Spurgeon, C. H. *An All-Round Ministry.* (Carlisle, PA: Banner of Truth Trust, 1978), 33.

[341] Zodhiates, S. *The Complete Word Study Dictionary: New Testament* (electronic ed.). (Chattanooga, TN: AMG Publishers, 2000).

[342] Wuest, K. S. *Wuest's Word Studies from the Greek New Testament: for the English Reader* (Vol. 12). (Grand Rapids: Eerdmans, 1997), 24.

[343] Spurgeon, C. H. *Lectures to My Students: Addresses Delivered to the Students of the Pastor's College, Metropolitan Tabernacle. Second series.* (Vol. 2). (New York: Robert Carter and Brothers, 1889), 165.

[344] Spurgeon, C. H. *An All-Round Ministry.* (Carlisle, PA: Banner of Truth Trust, 1978), 221–222.

[345] Spurgeon, C. H. "Holding Fast the Faith." Sermon delivered February 5, 1888, Metropolitan Tabernacle.

[346] Spurgeon, C. H. "Labouring and Not Fainting." Sermon delivered September 8, 1872, Metropolitan Tabernacle.

[347] Spurgeon, C. H. "Paul the Ready." Sermon delivered May 22, 1890, Metropolitan Tabernacle.

[348] Spurgeon, C. H. "Preach the Gospel." Sermon delivered August 5, 1855, New Park Street Chapel.

[349] Spurgeon, C. H. *An All-Round Ministry.* (Carlisle, PA: Banner of Truth Trust, 1978), 280.

[350] Spurgeon, C. H. "Prosperity Under Persecution." Sermon delivered 1872, Metropolitan Tabernacle.

[351] Exell, J. S. *The Biblical Illustrator: Revelation.* (New York; Chicago; Toronto; London; Edinburgh: Fleming H. Revell Company, n.d.), 229.

[352] Spurgeon, C. H. *The Sword and Trowel.* (August, 1887), 400.

[353] Spurgeon, C. H. "Feeding on the Word." Sermon delivered May 8, 1890, Metropolitan Tabernacle.

[354] Spurgeon, C. H. "The Cause and Cure of Weariness in Sabbath-School Teachers." Sermon delivered November 8, 1887, Metropolitan Tabernacle.

[355] from J. C. Ryle's little book *Spiritual Songs,* published in 1849. Adapted. Changed the word "Christian" to "man of God."

[356] Spurgeon, C. H. *Autobiography,* Volume 2: *The Full Harvest 1860–1892.* (Carlisle, PA: The Banner of Truth Trust, 1973), 501 (footnote entry).

[357] Spurgeon, C. H. *Lectures to My Students: Addresses Delivered to the Students of the Pastor's College, Metropolitan Tabernacle. Second series.* (Vol. 2). (New York: Robert Carter and Brothers, 1889), "The Minister's Fainting Fits."

[358] Amundsen, Darrel, "The Anguish and Agonies of Charles Spurgeon," https://christianhistoryinstitute.org/magazine/article/anguish-and-agonies-of-charles-spurgeon, accessed January 4, 2023.

[359] Williams, W. *Personal Reminiscences of Charles Haddon Spurgeon.* (London: The Gospel Tract Society, 1895), 40. Note: Spurgeon said, "I have been urged to preach on teetotalism, but I lay the axe at the root of the tree." Williams says, Spurgeon became an abstainer the last few years of his life and did more in denouncing strong drink than he had in his earlier years. See the same book, page 39.

[360] Spurgeon, C. H. "God's Firebrands." Sermon delivered at the Metropolitan Tabernacle, published January 19, 1911.

[361] Spurgeon, C. H. *An All-Round Ministry.* (Carlisle, PA: Banner of Truth Trust, 1978), 102.

[362] Ibid., 104.

[363] Ibid., 108.

[364] Charles Spurgeon Collection: Spurgeon, C. H. *John Ploughman's Talk.*

365 Spurgeon, C. H. *Eccentric Preachers*. (London: Passmore & Alabaster, 1879), 9.

366 Spurgeon, C. H. *Lectures to My Students: Addresses Delivered to the Students of the Pastor's College, Metropolitan Tabernacle. Second series.* (Vol. 2). (New York: Robert Carter and Brothers, 1889), 96.

367 Charles Spurgeon Collection: Spurgeon, C. H. *John Ploughman's Talk*.

368 Spurgeon, C. H. "Fencing the Table." Sermon delivered January 2, 1876, Metropolitan Tabernacle.

369 Spurgeon, C. H. "The Personality of the Holy Ghost." Sermon delivered January 21, 1855, New Park Street Chapel.

370 Spurgeon, C. H. "Christian Baptism." Sermon delivered April 19, 1861, Metropolitan Tabernacle.

371 *Spurgeon's Autobiography,* Vol. 1. (Fleming Revell Company, 1898), 154.

372 Spurgeon, C. H. "Fencing the Table." Sermon delivered January 2, 1876, Metropolitan Tabernacle.

373 Spurgeon, C. H. "Grappling Irons." Sermon delivered May 4, 1884, Metropolitan Tabernacle.

374 Spurgeon, C. H. "The Infallibility of Scripture." Sermon delivered March 11, 1888, Metropolitan Tabernacle.

375 Letter to the honorary secretary of the Church of England Burial, Funeral, and Mourning Reform Association, September 11, 1890.

376 Spurgeon, C. H. "Compassion on the Ignorant." Sermon delivered April 3, 1884, Metropolitan Tabernacle.

377 Spurgeon, C. H. *Come Ye Children*. (London: Passmore and Alabaster 1897), "Obtaining Our Lord's Heart for Loving and Teaching Children," Chapter Three.

378 Spurgeon, C. H. "The First Cry from the Cross." Sermon delivered October 24, 1869, Metropolitan Tabernacle.

379 Spurgeon, C. H. "The Head of the Church." Sermon delivered November 1, 1868, Metropolitan Tabernacle.

380 Spurgeon, C. H. "The First Sermon in the Tabernacle." Sermon delivered March 25, 1861, Metropolitan Tabernacle.

381 C.H. Spurgeon. "The Head of the Church." Sermon delivered November 1, 1868, Metropolitan Tabernacle.

382 Murray, Ian. *The Forgotten Spurgeon*. (Edinburgh: The Banner of Truth Trust, 1986), 240–249.

[383] Spurgeon, C. H. *Lectures to My Students: Addresses Delivered to the Students of the Pastor's College, Metropolitan Tabernacle. Second series.* (Vol. 2). (New York: Robert Carter and Brothers, 1889), 144.

[384] Spurgeon, C. H. *An All-Round Ministry.* (Carlisle, PA: Banner of Truth Trust, 1900/1960), 42–43.

[385] Spurgeon, C. H. *Lectures to My Students: Addresses Delivered to the Students of the Pastor's College, Metropolitan Tabernacle. Second series.* (Vol. 2). (New York: Robert Carter and Brothers, 1889), 245.

[386] Spurgeon, C. H. "The Church as She Should Be" (No. 984). Sermon delivered 1871, Metropolitan Tabernacle.

[387] *Sword and the Trowel,* February 1869, notes the six-step process for church membership.

[388] Spurgeon, C. H. "Grace Preferred to Gifts." Sermon delivered September 1, 1881, Metropolitan Tabernacle.

[389] Spurgeon, C. H. *Lectures to My Students: Addresses Delivered to the Students of the Pastor's College, Metropolitan Tabernacle. Second series.* (Vol. 2). (New York: Robert Carter and Brothers, 1889), 244.

[390] Spurgeon, Susannah and William Harrald. Autobiography of Charles H. Spurgeon Compiled from His Diary, Letters, and Records (Vol. 1). (1898), 393–394.

[391] Spurgeon, C. H. "Messengers Wanted." Sermon delivered April 22, 1866, Metropolitan Tabernacle.

[392] *Sword and the Trowel,* 1872:441

[393] Spurgeon, C. H. *Speeches at Home and Abroad.* (1878), 65.

[394] Spurgeon, C. H. "Church Increase." Sermon delivered August 18, 1881, Metropolitan Tabernacle.

[395] Spurgeon, C. H. *Lectures to my Students: Commenting and Commentaries; Lectures Addressed to the Students of the Pastor's College, Metropolitan Tabernacle,* (Vol. 4). (New York: Sheldon & Company, 1876), 4–5.

[396] Ibid., 11.

[397] Spurgeon, C. H. *Lectures to My Students: Addresses Delivered to the Students of the Pastor's College, Metropolitan Tabernacle. Second series.* (Vol. 2). (New York: Robert Carter and Brothers, 1889), 244.

[398] Ibid.

[399] Ibid.

[400] Ibid.

[401] From Spurgeon's letter to Mr. Near, February 22, 1890, Spurgeon's College.

402 Spurgeon, C. H. *Lectures to My Students: Addresses Delivered to the Students of the Pastor's College, Metropolitan Tabernacle. Second series.* (Vol. 2). (New York: Robert Carter and Brothers, 1889), 326.

403 Day, Richard E. *The Shadow of the Broad Brim.* (Lancaster, CA: Striving Together Publications, 2013), 173–174.

404 Spurgeon, C. H. *Lectures to My Students: Addresses Delivered to the Students of the Pastor's College, Metropolitan Tabernacle. Second series.* (Vol. 2). (New York: Robert Carter and Brothers, 1889), 245.

405 Spurgeon, C. H. *Autobiography,* Volume 2: *The Full Harvest 1860–1892.* (Carlisle, PA: The Banner of Truth Trust, 1973), 73.

406 Ibid., 74.

407 Spurgeon, C. H. "The Church—Conservative and Aggressive." Sermon delivered May 19, 1861, Metropolitan Tabernacle.

408 Spurgeon, C. H. *The Sword and Trowel.* (February, 1869), 149.

409 Spurgeon, C. H. *Autobiography,* Volume 2: *The Full Harvest 1860–1892.* (Carlisle, PA: The Banner of Truth Trust, 1973), 75.

410 Ibid.

411 Spurgeon, C. H. "Our Gifts, and How to Use Them." Sermon delivered in 1872, Metropolitan Tabernacle.

412 Spurgeon, C. H. "Are You Prepared to Die?" Sermon delivered, 1865, Metropolitan Tabernacle.

413 Spurgeon, C. H. *Morning and Evening.* (Great Britain: Christian Focus Publications, 1994), February 17 (Evening).

414 Spurgeon, C. H. "Confession of Sin: A Sermon with Seven Texts." Sermon delivered January 18, 1857, New Park Street Chapel.

415 Adcock, E. F. *Charles H. Spurgeon: Prince of Preachers.* (Anderson, Indiana: Gospel Tract Company, 1925), 112.

416 Spurgeon, C. H. *Lectures to My Students: Addresses Delivered to the Students of the Pastor's College, Metropolitan Tabernacle. Second series.* (Vol. 2). (New York: Robert Carter and Brothers, 1889), 155.

417 Ibid., 156.

418 Spurgeon, C. H. "Monday Address," May 19, 1879.

419 Amundsen, Darrel, "The Anguish and Agonies of Charles Spurgeon," https://christianhistoryinstitute.org/magazine/article/anguish-and-agonies-of-charles-spurgeon, accessed January 4, 2023.

420 Spurgeon, C. H. "Exceeding Gladness." Sermon delivered December 21, 1884, Metropolitan Tabernacle.

421 Spurgeon, C. H. *Morning and Evening.* (Great Britain: Christian Focus Publications, 1994), April 21 (Morning).

[422] Day, Richard E. *The Shadow of the Broad Brim.* (Lancaster, CA: Striving Together Publications, 2013), 60–61.

[423] Spurgeon, C. H. *Morning and Evening.* (Great Britain: Christian Focus Publications, 1994), July 17 (Morning).

[424] George, Timothy. *Baptist Theologians,* 274.

[425] Spurgeon, C. H. "Springtime in Nature and Grace." Sermon delivered May 1, 1887, Metropolitan Tabernacle.

[426] Spurgeon, C. H. "Strong Faith." Sermon delivered July 15, 1877, Metropolitan Tabernacle.

[427] C.H. Spurgeon. Believers Sent by Christ, As Christ Is Sent By the Father. Sermon delivered May 11, 1890, Metropolitan Tabernacle.

[428] Eric Hayden. The Unforgettable Spurgeon (Greenville, SC: The Emerald House Group, 1997), 124.

[429] Spurgeon, C. H. *The Sword and Trowel.* (January, 1880), Notes: Evangelists.

[430] Spurgeon, C. H. *Lectures to My Students: Addresses Delivered to the Students of the Pastor's College, Metropolitan Tabernacle. Second series.* (Vol. 2). (New York: Robert Carter and Brothers, 1889), 72.

[431] Ibid., 73.

[432] Spurgeon, C. H. *Lectures to my Students: Commenting and Commentaries; Lectures Addressed to the Students of the Pastor's College, Metropolitan Tabernacle,* (Vol. 4). (New York: Sheldon & Company, 1876), 4.

[433] Spurgeon, C. H. *Lectures to My Students: Addresses Delivered to the Students of the Pastor's College, Metropolitan Tabernacle. Second series.* (Vol. 2). (New York: Robert Carter and Brothers, 1889), 146–147.

[434] Spurgeon, C. H. *Lectures to My Students: Addresses Delivered to the Students of the Pastor's College, Metropolitan Tabernacle. Second series.* (Vol. 2). (New York: Robert Carter and Brothers, 1889), 144.

[435] Ibid., 140–141.

[436] Spurgeon, C. H. *Lectures to My Students: Addresses Delivered to the Students of the Pastor's College, Metropolitan Tabernacle. Second series.* (Vol. 2). (New York: Robert Carter and Brothers, 1889), 46.

[437] Spurgeon, C. H. *Faith's Checkbook,* October 4.

[438] Spurgeon, C. H. *Morning and Evening.* (Great Britain: Christian Focus Publications, 1994), November 19 (Morning).

[439] Spurgeon, C. H. *Lectures to My Students: Addresses Delivered to the Students of the Pastor's College, Metropolitan Tabernacle.* (Vol. 1). (London: Passmore and Alabaster, 1875), 183.

[440] Spurgeon, C. H. *An All-Round Ministry*. (Carlisle, PA: Banner of Truth Trust, 1978), 247.

[441] Spurgeon, C. H. *Lectures to My Students: Addresses Delivered to the Students of the Pastor's College, Metropolitan Tabernacle. Second series.* (Vol. 2). (New York: Robert Carter and Brothers, 1889), 169.

[442] Spurgeon, C. H. "Gathering to the Centre." Sermon delivered June 4, 1876, Metropolitan Tabernacle.

[443] Spurgeon, C. H. *The New Park Street Pulpit Sermons* (Vol. 2). (London: Passmore & Alabaster, 1856), vi.

[444] White, B. R. *The Baptist Quarterly*. "Charles Haddon Spurgeon: Educationalist," Part 2. https://biblicalstudies.org.uk/pdf/bq/32-2_073.pdf, accessed January 9, 2023.

[445] Spurgeon, C. H. *The Sword and the Trowel*. (London: Passmore & Alabaster, 1881), 133.

[446] Day, Richard E. *The Shadow of the Broad Brim*. (Lancaster, CA: Striving Together Publications, 2013), 121.

[447] Ibid., 116.

[448] Spurgeon, C. H. *Lectures to My Students: Addresses Delivered to the Students of the Pastor's College, Metropolitan Tabernacle. Second series.* (Vol. 2). (New York: Robert Carter and Brothers, 1889), 247.

[449] Spurgeon, C. H. *Speeches at Home and Abroad*. (1878), 65–66.

[450] Williams, W. *Personal Reminiscences of Charles Haddon Spurgeon*. (London: The Gospel Tract Society, 1895), 39.

[451] Spurgeon, C. H. "Facing the Wind." Sermon delivered September 28, 1876, Metropolitan Tabernacle.

[452] Spurgeon, C. H. "Wheat in the Barn." Published on Thursday, February 12, 1914, delivered at Metropolitan Tabernacle.

[453] Spurgeon, C. H. "The Destroyer Destroyed." Sermon delivered December 6, 1857, New Park Street Chapel.

[454] Fullerton, W. Y. *Charles H. Spurgeon, a Biography,* 118.

[455] Spurgeon, C. H. "The Resurrection of the Dead" (a sermon). February 17, 1856 (London: Passmore and Alabaster, 1857), 104.

[456] Spurgeon, C. H. "How to Read the Bible." Sermon delivered June 21, 1866, Metropolitan Tabernacle.

[457] Spurgeon, C. H. "Receiving the Holy Ghost." Sermon delivered July 13, 1884, Metropolitan Tabernacle.

[458] Spurgeon, C. H. "The Holy Ghost—The Great Teacher." Sermon delivered November 18, 1855, Metropolitan Tabernacle.

[459] Spurgeon, C. H. "Hearing with Heed." Sermon delivered August 9, 1885, Metropolitan Tabernacle.

[460] Spurgeon, C. H. *Autobiography,* Volume 2: *The Full Harvest 1860–1892.* (Carlisle, PA: The Banner of Truth Trust, 1973), 440.

[461] Ibid.

[462] Spurgeon, C. H. *Lectures to My Students: Addresses Delivered to the Students of the Pastor's College, Metropolitan Tabernacle. Second series.* (Vol. 2). (New York: Robert Carter and Brothers, 1889), 389.

[463] Spurgeon, C. H. *Lectures to My Students: The Art of Illustration; Addresses Delivered to the Students of the Pastor's College, Metropolitan Tabernacle,* (Vol. 3). (London: Passmore & Alabaster, 1905), 3.

[464] Ibid., 2.

[465] Spurgeon, C. H. "Feathers for Arrows: Or Illustrations for Preachers and Teachers, from My Note Book." (London: Passmore & Alabaster, 1870), Preface.

[466] Spurgeon, C. H. *Lectures to My Students: Addresses Delivered to the Students of the Pastor's College, Metropolitan Tabernacle. Second series.* (Vol. 2). (New York: Robert Carter and Brothers, 1889), 353.

[467] Ibid., 140–141.

[468] Spurgeon, C. H. "Christian Baptism." Sermon delivered April 19, 1861, Metropolitan Tabernacle.

[469] Spurgeon, C. H. *The Complete Works of C. H. Spurgeon: Volume 69: Autobiography Vol. 4,* Chapter 92.

[470] Spurgeon, C. H. "Receiving the Kingdom of God as a Little Child." Sermon delivered October 20, 1878, Metropolitan Tabernacle.

[471] Spurgeon, C. H. "Harvest Men Wanted." Sermon delivered August 17, 1873, Metropolitan Tabernacle.

[472] Ibid.

[473] Spurgeon, C. H. "A Plain Man's Sermon." Sermon delivered January 17, 1886, Metropolitan Tabernacle.

[474] Spurgeon, C. H. "Thanksgiving and Prayer." Sermon delivered September 27, 1863, Metropolitan Tabernacle.

[475] Spurgeon, C. H. "The Object of the Lord's Supper." Sermon delivered September 2, 1877, Metropolitan Tabernacle.

[476] Spurgeon, C. H. "The Right Observance of the Lord's Supper." Sermon delivered June 4, 1882, Metropolitan Tabernacle.

[477] Spurgeon, C. H. "Songs of Deliverance." Sermon delivered July 28, 1867, Metropolitan Tabernacle.

[478] Spurgeon, C. H. *Autobiography,* Volume 2: *The Full Harvest 1860–1892.* (Carlisle, PA: The Banner of Truth Trust, 1973), 316.

[479] Spurgeon, C. H. "The Greatest Exhibition of the Age." Sermon delivered May 5, 1889, Metropolitan Tabernacle.

[480] Spurgeon, C. H. "The Object of the Lord's Supper." Sermon delivered September 2, 1877, Metropolitan Tabernacle.

[481] Spurgeon, C. H. "Preparation Necessary for the Communion." Sermon delivered September 9, 1857, Metropolitan Tabernacle.

[482] Spurgeon, C. H. *The Soul Winner.* (Grand Rapids: Eerdmans, 1963), 19–20.

[483] Spurgeon, C. H. *Lectures to My Students: Addresses Delivered to the Students of the Pastor's College, Metropolitan Tabernacle. Second series.* (Vol. 2). (New York: Robert Carter and Brothers, 1889), 141.

[484] Spurgeon, C. H. *Autobiography,* Volume 2: *The Full Harvest 1860–1892.* (Carlisle, PA: The Banner of Truth Trust, 1973), 313.

[485] Spurgeon, C. H. "The Missionaries' Charge and Charta." Sermon delivered April 21, 1861, Metropolitan Tabernacle.

[486] Fullerton, W. Y. *Charles H. Spurgeon, a Biography,* A Chapter of Incidents.

[487] Spurgeon, C. H. *Come Ye Children.* (London: Passmore and Alabaster 1897), "The Children's Shepherd," Chapter 4.

[488] Spurgeon, C. H. *Lectures to My Students: Addresses Delivered to the Students of the Pastor's College, Metropolitan Tabernacle. Second series.* (Vol. 2). (New York: Robert Carter and Brothers, 1889), "The Misister's Self-Watch."

[489] Spurgeon, C. H. *An All-Round Ministry.* (Carlisle, PA: Banner of Truth Trust, 1978), 254.

[490] Spurgeon, C. H. *Lectures to My Students: Addresses Delivered to the Students of the Pastor's College, Metropolitan Tabernacle. Second series.* (Vol. 2). (New York: Robert Carter and Brothers, 1889), 168.

[491] Spurgeon, C. H. *Lectures to My Students: Addresses Delivered to the Students of the Pastor's College, Metropolitan Tabernacle.* (Vol. 1). (London: Passmore and Alabaster, 1875), 182.

[492] Spurgeon, C. H. *The Soul Winner: Qualifications for Soul-Winning—Manward.* (New Kensington, PA: Whitaker House, 1995), 72.

[493] Spurgeon, C. H. *Essential Works of Charles Spurgeon.* (Barbour Publishing, 2009), 1428.

[494] Spurgeon, Susannah and William Harrald. Autobiography of Charles H. Spurgeon Compiled from His Diary, Letters, and Records (Vol. 1). (1898), 356.

[495] Ibid., 327.

[496] Spurgeon, C. H. "Saving Faith." Sermon delivered March 15, 1884, Metropolitan Tabernacle.

[497] Spurgeon, C. H. *Lectures to My Students: Addresses Delivered to the Students of the Pastor's College, Metropolitan Tabernacle. Second series.* (Vol. 2). (New York: Robert Carter and Brothers, 1889), 59.

[498] Young, Dinsdale T. *C. H. Spurgeon's Prayers.* (London: Passmore & Alabaster, 1905), v, viii.

[499] Spurgeon, C. H. *Lectures to My Students: Addresses Delivered to the Students of the Pastor's College, Metropolitan Tabernacle. Second series.* (Vol. 2). (New York: Robert Carter and Brothers, 1889), 58.

[500] Spurgeon, C. H. *Lectures to My Students: Addresses Delivered to the Students of the Pastor's College, Metropolitan Tabernacle. Second series.* (Vol. 2). (New York: Robert Carter and Brothers, 1889), 33.

[501] Ibid., 69.

[502] Ibid., 68–69.

[503] Ibid., 55–56.

[504] Spurgeon, C. H. *Lectures to My Students: Addresses Delivered to the Students of the Pastor's College, Metropolitan Tabernacle. Second series.* (Vol. 2). (New York: Robert Carter and Brothers, 1889), 20.

[505] Spurgeon, C. H. *An All-Round Ministry.* (Carlisle, PA: Banner of Truth Trust, 1978), 236.

[506] Spurgeon, C. H. *Lectures to My Students: Addresses Delivered to the Students of the Pastor's College, Metropolitan Tabernacle. Second series.* (Vol. 2). (New York: Robert Carter and Brothers, 1889), 216.

[507] Spurgeon, C. H. *Morning and Evening.* (Great Britain: Christian Focus Publications, 1994), Jan. 30 (Morning).

[508] Spurgeon, C. H. *Lectures to My Students: Addresses Delivered to the Students of the Pastor's College, Metropolitan Tabernacle. Second series.* (Vol. 2). (New York: Robert Carter and Brothers, 1889), 93.

[509] Ibid., 156.

[510] Spurgeon, C. H. *An All-Round Ministry.* (Carlisle, PA: Banner of Truth Trust, 1978), 355.

[511] *Harper's New Monthly Magazine.* (New York: Harper and Brothers Publishers, December, 1870–May, 1871, Vol. XLII), 798.

[512] Spurgeon, C. H. *The Soul Winner.* (Grand Rapids: Eerdmans, 1963), 140.

[513] Spurgeon, C. H. "Out of Egypt." Sermon delivered August 20, 1882, Metropolitan Tabernacle.

[514] Spurgeon, C. H. "Receiving the Kingdom of God as a Little Child." Sermon delivered October 20, 1878, Metropolitan Tabernacle.

[515] Spurgeon, C. H. *Lectures to My Students: Addresses Delivered to the Students of the Pastor's College, Metropolitan Tabernacle. Second series.* (Vol. 2). (New York: Robert Carter and Brothers, 1889), 95.

[516] Ibid.

[517] Spurgeon, C. H. *Faith's Checkbook,* November 16.

[518] Spurgeon, C. H. "The Candle." Sermon delivered April 24, 1881, Metropolitan Tabernacle.

[519] Spurgeon, C. H. *The Sword and Trowel.* (July, 1876), "The Power of Nonconformity."

[520] Spurgeon, C. H. *The Sword and Trowel.* (March, 1873), "A Political Dissenter."

[521] Ibid.

[522] Spurgeon, C. H. *The Sword and the Trowel.* (London: Passmore & Alabaster, 1873), March.

[523] Spurgeon, C. H. *Autobiography, Vol. 1: The Early Years 1834-1859.* (London: Passmore & Alabaster, 1897), Chapter 81.

[524] Spurgeon, C. H. *Lectures to My Students: Addresses Delivered to the Students of the Pastor's College, Metropolitan Tabernacle. Second series.* (Vol. 2). (New York: Robert Carter and Brothers, 1889), 330–331.

[525] Spurgeon, C. H. "Write the Name of Jesus on Your Crosses." *Sword and the Trowel,* 1884. Sermon delivered at a Prayer Meeting, Metropolitan Tabernacle, 473; and in the sermon, "Gathering to the Centre." Sermon delivered June 4, 1876, Metropolitan Tabernacle.

[526] Spurgeon, C. H. *Lectures to My Students: Addresses Delivered to the Students of the Pastor's College, Metropolitan Tabernacle. Second series.* (Vol. 2). (New York: Robert Carter and Brothers, 1889), 196.

[527] Davenport, Henry. *Life and Works of Charles H. Spurgeon.* (Memorial Publishing Co., 1892), 525–526.

[528] Spurgeon, C. H. "The Superlative Excellence of the Holy Spirit." Sermon delivered June 12, 1864, Metropolitan Tabernacle.

[529] Spurgeon, C. H. *The Soul Winner.* (Grand Rapids: Eerdmans, 1963), 120–121

[530] Spurgeon, C. H. *Autobiography,* Volume 2: *The Full Harvest 1860–1892.* (Carlisle, PA: The Banner of Truth Trust, 1973), 322.

[531] Spurgeon, C. H. *The New Park Street Pulpit Sermons* (Vol. 2). (London: Passmore & Alabaster, 1856), 23.

[532] Spurgeon, C. H. "Hearing with Heed." Sermon delivered August 9, 1885, Metropolitan Tabernacle.

[533] Spurgeon, C. H. *Lectures to My Students: Addresses Delivered to the Students of the Pastor's College, Metropolitan Tabernacle. Second series.* (Vol. 2). (New York: Robert Carter and Brothers, 1889), 220.

[534] Spurgeon, C. H. "The Infallibility of Scripture." Sermon delivered March 11, 1888, Metropolitan Tabernacle.

[535] Spurgeon, C. H. *Lectures to My Students: Addresses Delivered to the Students of the Pastor's College, Metropolitan Tabernacle. Second series.* (Vol. 2). (New York: Robert Carter and Brothers, 1889), 78.

[536] Ibid., 267.

[537] Ibid., 265.

[538] Spurgeon, C. H. *Spurgeon's Sermons on Soulwinning.* (Grand Rapids: Kregel, 1995), 99–100.

[539] Sorenson, Austin L. "The Pulpit and the Pew." *The Sword of the Lord,* Nov. 7, 2003.

[540] Spurgeon, C. H. *Lectures to My Students: Addresses Delivered to the Students of the Pastor's College, Metropolitan Tabernacle. Second series.* (Vol. 2). (New York: Robert Carter and Brothers, 1889), 350.

[541] Spurgeon, Susannah and William Harrald. Autobiography of Charles H. Spurgeon Compiled from His Diary, Letters, and Records (Vol. 2). (1898), 381.

[542] Spurgeon, C. H. "Paul—His Cloak and His Books." Sermon delivered November 29, 1863, Metropolitan Tabernacle.

[543] Spurgeon, C. H. *Lectures to My Students: The 28 Lectures, Complete and Unabridged—A Spiritual Classic of Christian Wisdom, Prayer and Preaching in the Ministry.* (Scotts Valley, CA: CreateSpace, 2018), 138.

[544] Spurgeon, C. H. "How to Read the Bible." Sermon delivered June 21, 1866, Metropolitan Tabernacle.

[545] Spurgeon, C. H. "Paul—His Cloak and His Books." Sermon delivered November 29, 1863, Metropolitan Tabernacle.

[546] Ibid.

[547] Ibid.

[548] Spurgeon, C. H. *Autobiography,* Volume 2: *The Full Harvest 1860–1892.* (Carlisle, PA: The Banner of Truth Trust, 1973), 274.

[549] Ibid., 420.

[550] Day, Richard E. *The Shadow of the Broad Brim.* (Lancaster, CA: Striving Together Publications, 2013), 107.

[551] Spurgeon, C. H. "Paul—His Cloak and His Books." Sermon delivered November 29, 1863, Metropolitan Tabernacle.

[552] Spurgeon, C. H. "An Exciting Enquiry." Sermon delivered at Metropolitan Tabernacle, and published March 26, 1908.

[553] Spurgeon, C. H. *Autobiography, Vol. 1: The Early Years 1834-1859.* (London: Passmore & Alabaster, 1897), 9.

[554] Spurgeon, C. H. "Assured Security in Christ." Sermon delivered January 2, 1870, Metropolitan Tabernacle.

[555] Spurgeon, C. H. "Feathers for Arrows: Or Illustrations for Preachers and Teachers, from My Note Book." (London: Passmore & Alabaster, 1870), 1.

[556] Spurgeon, C. H. *An All-Round Ministry.* (Carlisle, PA: Banner of Truth Trust, 1978), 369.

[557] Spurgeon, C. H. "A Caution to the Presumptuous." Sermon delivered May 13 1855, New Park Street Chapel.

[558] Spurgeon, C. H. *Lectures to My Students: Addresses Delivered to the Students of the Pastor's College, Metropolitan Tabernacle. Second series.* (Vol. 2). (New York: Robert Carter and Brothers, 1889), 13-14.

[559] Spurgeon, Susannah and William Harrald. Autobiography of Charles H. Spurgeon Compiled from His Diary, Letters, and Records (Vol. 1). (1898), 323.

[560] Spurgeon, C. H. *Lectures to My Students: Addresses Delivered to the Students of the Pastor's College, Metropolitan Tabernacle. Second series.* (Vol. 2). (New York: Robert Carter and Brothers, 1889), 282.

[561] Spurgeon, C. H. "Spiritual Revival, the Want of the Church." Sermon delivered November 11, 1856, Metropolitan Tabernacle.

[562] Spurgeon, C. H. "Enquire of the Lord." Sermon delivered July 9, 1876, Metropolitan Tabernacle.

[563] Spurgeon, C. H. "The Great Revival." Sermon preached March 28, 1858, New Park Street Chapel.

[564] Spurgeon, C. H. "Gathering to the Centre." Sermon delivered June 4, 1876, Metropolitan Tabernacle.

[565] Spurgeon, Susannah and William Harrald. Autobiography of Charles H. Spurgeon Compiled from His Diary, Letters, and Records (Vol. 1). (1898), 172.

[566] Spurgeon, C. H. *Lectures to My Students: Addresses Delivered to the Students of the Pastor's College, Metropolitan Tabernacle. Second series.* (Vol. 2). (New York: Robert Carter and Brothers, 1889), 245.

[567] Ray, Charles. Charles Haddon Spurgeon. (London: Passmore & Alabaster, 1903), 358.

[568] Spurgeon, C. H. "On Ministers." From an address at the Baptist Union at Cambridge. *The Christian's Penny Magazine.* (London: John Snow & Company, 1871), 136.

[569] "Ordination Variations: Some Wonder Is It Baptistic? Is It Biblical?" ABP NEWS, March 16, 2006. https://baptistnews.com/article/ordination-variations-some-wonder-is-it-baptistic-is-it-biblical/, accessed January 11, 2023.

[570] Spurgeon, Susannah and William Harrald. Autobiography of Charles H. Spurgeon Compiled from His Diary, Letters, and Records (Vol. 1). (1898), 172.

[571] Spurgeon, C. H. "Paul—His Cloak and His Books." Sermon delivered November 29, 1863, Metropolitan Tabernacle.

[572] George, Christian. *Beeson Podcast,* Episode 383. March 13, 2018.

[573] Spurgeon, C. H. *Lectures to My Students.* (Grand Rapids: Zondervan, 1970), 226.

[574] Spurgeon, C. H. *The Soul Winner.* (Grand Rapids: Eerdmans, 1963), 223.

[575] Spurgeon, C. H. *Lectures to My Students.* (Grand Rapids: Zondervan, 1970), 209.

[576] Ibid., 91–92.

[577] Spurgeon, Susannah and William Harrald. Autobiography of Charles H. Spurgeon Compiled from His Diary, Letters, and Records (Vol. 1). (1898), 398.

[578] Spurgeon, C. H. *Autobiography,* Volume 2: *The Full Harvest 1860–1892.* (Carlisle, PA: The Banner of Truth Trust, 1973), 311–312.

[579] Spurgeon, C. H. *Lectures to My Students: A Selection from Addresses Delivered to the Students of the Pastor's College, Metropolitan Tabernacle,* (Vol. 1). (London: Passmore and Alabaster, 1875), 88.

[580] Spurgeon, C. H. *Lectures to My Students.* (Grand Rapids: Zondervan, 1970), 85.

[581] Spurgeon, C. H. *An All-Round Ministry.* (Carlisle, PA: Banner of Truth Trust, 1978), 336.

582 Day, Richard E. *The Shadow of the Broad Brim.* (Lancaster, CA: Striving Together Publications, 2013), 114 (All but the first sentence, which comes from W. Y. Fullerton).

583 Spurgeon, C. H. *Autobiography,* Volume 2: *The Full Harvest 1860–1892.* (Carlisle, PA: The Banner of Truth Trust, 1973), 272.

584 Spurgeon, Thomas. Introduction to Spurgeon's lecture "What the Stones Say." https://www.gracegems.org/Spurgeon/what_the_stones_say.htm, accessed January 4, 2023.

585 Spurgeon, C. H. *Lectures to My Students.* (Grand Rapids: Zondervan, 1970), 134–135.

586 Ibid., 135.

587 Ibid., 94–95.

588 Spurgeon, Charles. *Lectures to My Students.* (Carlisle, PA: Banner of Truth Trust, 1875/2008), "On the Choice of a Text," 103–104.

589 Spurgeon, C. H. "The Evil and its Remedy." Sermon delivered November14, 1858, New Park Street Chapel.

590 Spurgeon, Susannah. *A Basket of Summer Fruit,* "Thanksgiving Street."

591 Day, Richard E. *The Shadow of the Broad Brim.* (Lancaster, CA: Striving Together Publications, 2013), 143.

592 Ibid., 144.

593 Spurgeon, C. H. "A Prayer for Everyone." Sermon delivered August 23, 1883, Metropolitan Tabernacle.

594 Spurgeon, C. H. *Autobiography,* Chapter XLV, 131.

595 Spurgeon, C. H. "How to Read the Bible." Sermon delivered June 21, 1866, Metropolitan Tabernacle.

596 Spurgeon, C. H. *The Soul Winner.* (Grand Rapids: Eerdmans, 1963), 125.

597 Packer, J. I. *InterVarsity Press*, "Evangelism and the Sovereignty of God," January 2012 Edition, 40.

598 Carlile, J.C. C. H. Spurgeon: An Interpretative Biography. (London: The Religious Tract Society and The Kingsgate Press, 1934), 297.

599 Spurgeon, C. H. "How to Read the Bible." Sermon delivered June 21, 1866, Metropolitan Tabernacle.

600 Spurgeon, C. H. *An All-Round Ministry.* (Carlisle, PA: Banner of Truth Trust, 1978), 234.

[601] Spurgeon, C. H. *Lectures to My Students: Addresses Delivered to the Students of the Pastor's College, Metropolitan Tabernacle. Second series.* (Vol. 2). (New York: Robert Carter and Brothers, 1889), 249.

[602] Ibid., 251.

[603] Spurgeon, C. H. *Lectures to My Students.* (Grand Rapids: Zondervan, 1970), 326–327.

[604] Spurgeon, C. H. "Personal Service." Sermon delivered May 3, 1860, at Surrey Chapel, BlackFriar's Road.

[605] Spurgeon, C. H. *The Sword and the Trowel.* (London: Passmore & Alabaster, 1878), September.

[606] Spurgeon, C. H. *The Christian's Penny Magazine.* (London: John Snow & Company, 1871), "On Ministers." From an address at the Baptist Union at Cambridge, 136.

[607] Chang, Geoff. "Learning the Art of Pastoring with C. H. Spurgeon," February 21, 2022.

[608] Spurgeon, C. H. *Lectures to My Students.* (Grand Rapids: Zondervan, 1970), 66.

[609] Spurgeon, C. H. *Autobiography,* Volume 2: *The Full Harvest 1860–1892.* (Carlisle, PA: The Banner of Truth Trust, 1973), 314.

[610] Spurgeon, C. H. "The Personality of the Holy Ghost." Sermon delivered January 21, 1855, New Park Street Chapel.

[611] Spurgeon, C. H. "Watching to See." Sermon delivered January 26, 1882, Metropolitan Tabernacle.

[612] Spurgeon, Susannah and William Harrald. Autobiography of Charles H. Spurgeon Compiled from His Diary, Letters, and Records (Vol. 1). (1898), 6.

[613] Spurgeon, C. H. *Morning and Evening.* (Great Britain: Christian Focus Publications, 1994), May 29 (Evening).

[614] Spurgeon, Susannah and William Harrald. Autobiography of Charles H. Spurgeon Compiled from His Diary, Letters, and Records (Vol. 1). (1898), 134.

[615] Spurgeon, C. H. *An All-Round Ministry.* (Carlisle, PA: Banner of Truth Trust, 1978), 363.

www.ingramcontent.com/pod-product-compliance
Lightning Source LLC
Chambersburg PA
CBHW031252090426
42742CB00007B/419